T0094708

a

America

aloging-in-Publication Data is

-6

ss.com

Th

B

Print

Librar ress
availa quest.

ISBN

40-4

www. re

DIAMON

Published in 2012 by Diamond Cutter Press

Book design by Clare Cerullo

Printed in the United States of America

Library of Congress Cataloging-in-Publication Data is
available upon request.

ISBN 978-1-9371140-4-6

www.diamondcutterpress.com

How the Root of Kindness Works

The Virtue That Benefits Others

Janet Kathleen Ettele

DIAMOND CUTTER PRESS

Dedicated with endless love to my mother,
Rosamond Patricia Elliot Ettele Sullivan,
and to all mothers who offer life's first touch of
loving-kindness.

Introduction

A Guide to the Bodhisattva's Way of Life (Bodhichayavatara) was first taught by Master Shantideva in India during the eighth century. He was born a prince, but chose the life of a monk and studied at Nalanda University. While at Nalanda, Master Shantideva appeared to do nothing but sleep, eat, and other necessary functions of the body and was perceived by the other monks to be an embarrassment to their prestigious university. The monks resented him for his laziness, and since there were rules that prevented them from having him expelled, they designed a plan they believed would be a perfect way to shame him into voluntarily leaving Nalanda. The plan included ordering him to give a public teaching. They thought that certainly he would realize that since he knew nothing and had nothing of value to teach, he would run away to avoid humiliation.

In the center of a field, they prepared a very high throne for him to teach from and invited people from all the surrounding areas to attend. To increase the challenge, they asked him to teach something that had never been taught before. Determined to leave no stone unturned in their effort to humiliate him, they had built the throne with no stairs by which to reach its seat. When Shantideva approached the throne, he placed his hand on its side and was immediately transported to the seat of the throne. Then, Shantideva proceeded to speak eloquently and spontaneously, reciting the Bodhichayavatara, which is now one of the most renowned texts in Buddhism. To the astonishment of those in attendance, the profound teaching flowed from Shantideva in the form of song-like poetry. It has been said that when Master Shantideva reached the final chapter on the Perfection of Wisdom, that his body raised higher and higher from the seat of the throne until he eventually disappeared from sight. His teachings continued, but his voice could only be heard by those who, having attained higher realizations in their own minds, had the ability to hear them.

A Guide to the Bodhisattva's Way of Life has provided students of the Buddhist Dharma from that day forward with what is commonly known as the Six Paramitas, or the Six Perfections. The Six Perfections provide the necessary guidance on how a Bodhisattva, motivated by compassion and the intention to benefit all beings, must perfect his or her mind on the path to enlightenment. For ordinary people like most of us, the verses provide the perfect guidance to live happy and meaningful lives.

How the Root of Kindness Works is based on the second of Master Shantideva's Six Perfections. Commonly translated as "Guarding Alertness" or "Moral and Ethical Discipline," the second perfection is the root of all good qualities providing the conduit for enlightenment—the foundation for a peaceful mind. Understanding that there are actions of body, speech, and mind that cause harm to ourselves and to others, we recognize the importance of cultivating mindfulness to guard against these harmful actions. This perfection also teaches us that by engaging in actions that bring benefit to others, we can purify the seeds of negativity that disturb our peace and happiness. The virtuous intention to help all sentient beings with a motivation of compassion and the practice of moral and ethical discipline is the root of kindness.

How the Root of Kindness Works continues in the style of *How Generosity Works*. Verses from Master Shantideva's teaching on Moral and Ethical Discipline are woven within the story to highlight their essence. With the wish for Master Shantideva's wisdom to meaningfully resonate in the world today, I offer this contemporary fable to link the wisdom from the past to the needs of the present.

For these very reasons, the Buddha has said
That as difficult as it is for a turtle to insert its neck
Into a yoke adrift upon the vast ocean,
It is more difficult to attain the human state.

IV. 20

Maggie had a thing for second-hand shops. Not pretentious antique shops with stuffy, creaky owners who peer over their glasses, appraising the value of each customer before extending either a cool or gracious greeting. She told Troy that the real treasures are found in the old industrial towns that outlived their glory days and somehow survived without reviving their industries. They live on, with a slow and steady pulse, in a freeze-framed sense of time.

Maggie's favorite shop was on Center Street, a winding road that followed the contour of the river, past the old mill that stopped running at least fifty years ago. A wooden sign painted with the words "Olde and Older" marked the turn where they pulled into a dirt parking area. It was late March in New England, and one of the first days that brought the smell of spring in the air and the last of the snow melting into muddy lawns. Abe, the owner, was pulling old bureaus, tables, and chairs outside to display in front of the store. He was a large man in his sixties with the smile of a young man who was neglecting to age. He turned briefly to watch the blue truck drive in, and then arranged the pieces of furniture hoping to attract customers.

"Abe!" Maggie called from across the lot. She took Troy by the hand. "Come on, Troy, you've gotta meet Abe. You'll love him."

Sunlight splashed off the dusty windowpanes behind where Abe stood, wiping his forehead with the red bandana he had taken from his jacket pocket. "Maggie?" He began walking towards them. He held his arms out to receive the hug she ran to give him. "I haven't seen you in months." He placed his hands on her shoulders and looked at her like a father might look at his daughter, and then asked, "Who is this fellow you've brought with you?"

"Abe, I'd like you to meet Troy. Troy, this is Abe." She tried to remember the rules of introduction, and hoped she had followed the proper sequence by first introducing the younger to the older person. Neither Troy nor Abe would have cared, but she did. She adored Abe and wanted to be sure he was given the appropriate respect.

Troy felt his hand disappear within Abe's massive grip when they shook hands. "Nice to meet you," he said.

"Likewise," said Abe.

Troy had the sense that within one handshake and one word, Abe had taken in everything there was to know about him. "Maggie told me you have the best shop around," Troy said.

"Well, there's not much you can't find here if you look hard enough." Abe rested his hand on Troy's back. "Take a look around if you'd like."

Troy stepped over puddles to look with polite interest at the pieces Abe had set outside. He listened as Maggie began to tell Abe about the classes she was taking at school, and then he turned to walk into the shop. Their voices faded as the door closed behind him, and Troy entered the musty smell of memories in cabinet drawers, pages of books, and upholstered chairs with intricately carved wood trim and curved legs. His hand brushed the surface of each piece of furniture he passed, leaving a wavy trail from his fingers streaked in the dust. He wondered how many families held hands around the dining room tables, or what conversations might have been shared from the armchairs. He had a tendency to romanticize family unity, and he pushed away the lump in his heart whenever he began longing for what he imagined a loving family might be. He squeezed between a sofa and a bookshelf to work his way over to the other side of the room where, in the far corner, he saw a brown guitar case leaning against the wall. He nearly knocked over a glass lamp when he reached to lift the case by its leather handle. He could tell by its weight that it wasn't empty, and with the hopeful anticipation of a childhood Christmas morning, he cleared a space on an old steamer trunk to set the case down flat. He opened the stiff latches and raised the lid. Pink velvet lined the case where the black-bodied guitar appeared to have been in a half-century sleep. At the top of the headstock was the famous Gibson logo, and above the fret board, Les Paul's signature was stamped in gold. Even though Troy already owned two guitars, he always kept an eye out for other guitars that could add different qualities of tone and texture to the music he played. He knew that Les Paul had been significant in the development of the solid-body electric guitar that made the sound of rock and roll possible. From his own perspective, Les Paul was a founding father for Troy's musical world.

The velvet in the lid of the case bore a matted imprint of the guitar's body, complete with outlines of knobs, strings, mother of pearl inlays, and tuning pegs. He lifted the guitar from its case and held it horizontally, with the bottom of the guitar eye level to check for warping in the neck. From this view, it looked straight. Even with the tarnished gold hardware, dents on the edge of the body, and a cigarette burn on the back, it was a beautiful guitar. He played the low E string and tuned it to the pitch he held as a constant reference in his mind, and continued tuning the other strings. The strings were old, but even so, the mahogany body produced a rich, mellow tone, which Troy could only imagine as golden when amplified. There was no price on the guitar case, and as far as he could see, there were no prices on anything in Abe's store. He put the guitar back in its case, closed the latches, and then pulled a wallet from his back pocket. He counted two twenties, a five, and four one dollar bills in the billfold. He put the wallet back in his pocket, and looked at the guitar case while mentally searching his truck for stashes of change and tip money he earned at the diner. It was his built-in savings plan to discreetly hide folded up bills in the glove compartment, or under the floor mats of his truck. He thought it safer to have multiple hiding places so, if ever discovered by a thief, not all would be lost. The biggest flaw in his system was that once hidden, he forgot about both the money and its location.

He carried the guitar in its case outside and walked to where Maggie and Abe were sitting in chairs, appearing to be human props in Abe's display. The sun was a soothing tonic after the long, hard winter they had just endured, and most everyone was outdoors soaking it up. People were washing mud from their cars and sweeping sand from sidewalks. Protected by the sun and wind moving through their hair, fearless children made mothers nervous riding their bikes without helmets.

Abe watched Troy walk towards them. "Pull up a chair and show us what you found."

Troy stood the guitar case on its end and leaned it against the chair where Maggie sat next to Abe. The sunlight exposed patches of mildew that spotted the case and a cobweb stretched across its base. Troy found a footstool and carried it over to join Abe and Maggie.

"This guitar has been in my shop for at least three months," Abe said, resting his hand on the case. "I don't think anyone's so much as touched it since it's been here. It came from the Deegan's home about five miles from town. You see, sometimes when the last person to live in a home dies, the family members that are still around go through the house and take the things they want. Then, I'll get a call from the lawyer handling the estate to come and take what's left behind. I've been around a long time, so all the lawyers in the area know about me." He leaned over to pick up a piece of paper that the wind had tossed on the ground in front of him and put it in his pocket. "Everyone's happy—the family gets money for things they don't want, the house is emptied for them so they can do whatever they're gonna do with the house, and everyone moves on. All the furniture, knick-knacks, and books move on too." His eyes caught the sunlight when he laughed and said, "No clothes though. I don't want to be bothered with folding and hanging clothes." Abe looked the case over and brushed the cobweb off it with his hand. "So, let's see what's inside this thing." He turned the case to reach its handle and passed it lightly to Troy. In Abe's hand, it looked weightless.

Troy balanced the case across his lap and lifted the latches. Abe's eyes weren't on the guitar or the case, but were watching the way Troy handled the guitar, lifting it with the careful steadiness one might lift a sleeping child.

"Troy, it's gorgeous," Maggie said as she helped him move the case onto the ground so he could hold the guitar.

"Isn't it?" Troy looked at Maggie and smiled. "When I first saw it, it was kinda like when I first saw you, Mags—love at first sight." He played a series of chords, tuning the strings between strums. "Judging by the weight of this, I'm guessing it could be one of the older models built before Gibson figured out how to make their guitars lighter." He wanted to enjoy the sensation of holding and playing the guitar before hearing the price. A guitar like this could command a lot more money than he had, so as long as the price was unknown, he felt the fullness of possibility.

"The Deegans had a son who was killed in Vietnam," Abe said. He lowered his eyes and scratched at some dried paint that had dripped onto the leg of his pants. "I didn't know him, but I remember hearing about his death when the news came home." He squinted to the sky, visiting a time that would feel like the present if he allowed himself to linger there. He cleared his throat and brought his attention back to Troy. "When we moved everything out of the house, one of the relatives told me the guitar belonged to that son and that it had stayed in his room, undisturbed, for decades."

Troy stopped playing the guitar and held it while he examined it more closely. His fingers gently rubbed the dings, scuffmarks, and the cigarette burn on the back of the guitar. Vietnam was a war that was over long before he was born, but he was aware of the battles that were still being fought in the minds and hearts of some of the older people he had grown up around. If a spirit exists that continues on after death, he wondered, might the young man whose guitar he was holding be more at peace now than many of the soldiers who had returned home? He hoped so.

"Troy," Abe said, "the guy who helps me is away, and I've got a house to empty. I need an extra pair of hands and a strong back. If you help me with the job, the guitar is yours."

"Seriously?" Troy asked and then was immediately embarrassed by his response. He didn't want to seem overly eager and was concerned that the value of the guitar was greater than the work Abe was asking for in exchange. "Of course I'll help you," he answered. "But I want to do more than that if I'm going to pay for the guitar by working." He turned to look at the shop and asked, "What else can I help you with?"

Abe laughed. "You have no idea how many loads we'll be carrying out of that house." He reassured Troy, "You'll be earning every penny that guitar is worth."

"Okay. When do you need me?" Troy asked.

"I'd like to have it done by the end of next week," Abe said. "What days are you free?"

"I have classes on Monday and Wednesday nights, but my schedule at the diner changes from week to week." Troy opened the case and carefully lowered the guitar into it. "I can let you know tomorrow." He closed all the latches around the case and leaned it against a small table next to Abe. He took his cell phone from his jacket pocket to add Abe's phone number into his directory. "What's your number?" he asked.

Before he spoke, Abe eyed Troy like a golfer might examine his next shot on the golf course. "Cell phones and pieces of paper get lost, but you're young, and I don't think you're at risk of losing your mind." His delivery had the blend of someone telling a joke and being dead serious at the same time. "So, put the phone back in your pocket, and I'll tell you my phone number."

Troy smiled at the challenge, closed the cover of the phone, and stuffed it back into his pocket. He sat up straight in his chair and drummed an abbreviated drum roll on his thighs. "Okay," he said. "I'm ready." Troy didn't realize it yet, but Abe was about to begin teaching him more than how to memorize a phone number.

Those who wish to guard their practice
Should very attentively guard their minds,
For those who do not guard their minds
Will be unable to guard their practice.

V. 1

The wheels of the truck kicked up gravel as Troy accelerated to make the turn onto Center Street. "It kinda freaked me out when Abe made me memorize his phone number."

Maggie laughed. "Abe wouldn't hurt a soul, but I know what you mean—he does have a certain way about him. I'm not sure what it is, but when I first met him, I suddenly became ridiculously shy. He's so damn sweet though that I got over it pretty quick."

Troy leaned over to open the glove compartment. "Maggie, there's a pen in there. Can you find it?" While she searched for a pen, he fished around under the seat, pulled out a small brown paper bag, and handed it to Maggie. "Just in case, write this down before I forget, okay?" He waited for her to have the pen ready to write and rattled off Abe's phone number while it was still fresh in his mind.

"Cheater!" Maggie laughed. She swatted his arm with the bag before she started writing. "I'll write it down, but I'm not giving it to you. If Abe asked you to memorize something, I wouldn't mess with him. I think there's always a reason for everything he does. So, just make sure you remember the number."

"Okay—deal," Troy said. "Just don't lose it." They were quiet while Maggie folded the bag with the phone number written on it and tucked it away in her purse, and Troy mentally recited the phone number over and over again. They had grown comfortable with stretches of silence. It wasn't that they knew everything there was to know about each other, but silence felt good when all was well and they could just enjoy quietly spending time together.

Maggie and Troy first met in December at the diner where they worked together. Troy was smitten with Maggie the moment he saw her. But Maggie hadn't paid much attention to him until a cold day in January when she saw him rush outside to give a bag filled with food to a homeless man. They had been clearing tables by the window facing the sidewalk when Troy saw the man push a shopping cart past the restaurant, collecting empty bottles and soda cans. He moved so quickly into the kitchen to fill a bag with food and then out the door that it seemed to Maggie he must have somehow known the man was on his way and that Troy was just waiting for him to show up. That was when she became equally smitten.

Troy invited Maggie to take a walk in the woods with him one day when their shift ended. It was a day after a snowstorm, and the woods were deep in freshly fallen snow. As they walked, their conversation was lively, and their voices seemed to follow them closely as if they were contained in an invisible and private soundproof booth that glided along with each step. Maggie told Troy that snowfalls remind her of how life flows. Countless tiny crystals—each unique from the other—fall one by one, but ultimately dissolve into one another. "All of nature is like that," she said, "a dance of form that is always changing." She wasn't sure about God or some almighty spirit but was certain that there in the woods, she could feel the presence of something unseen that felt primordial and wise. She hoped she wasn't just imagining it and that a silent law of nature might actually allow her to absorb some of that wisdom into herself just by breathing in the scent of pine and wood that filled the air.

Maggie's insistence that Troy take Abe's instruction seriously reminded him of their conversation that afternoon in the woods. He discovered that even though her smile had the ability to weaken his knees, her mind had the ability to inspire him. He appreciated the way she would bring any situation or challenge under the microscope of nature. Like a scientist might put a substance on a slide to examine it, Maggie examined problems and distilled them down to their simplest essence by finding a parallel in nature. "There's a give and take in nature that maintains its balance," she had told him, "and if you keep that in mind, then you'll strive to be kind and generous with what you give and careful with what you take." Talk wasn't cheap for Maggie. She lived by what she said, and at the risk of being hurt or let down, she assumed others would do the same.

Close to home, cars and trucks had turned their headlights on and the sky darkened into evening. A bank of clouds formed and swelled like a set of drapes sliding across the horizon. Troy wasn't ready to say goodnight to Maggie, and he wanted to postpone going back to his father's house as long as possible. His relationship with his father's wife, Maureen, was tense and walking into the house was like entering a minefield; he never knew what might set her off. Grace, his music teacher, had shared insights with Troy that strengthened his ability to not react with anger when Maureen was accusatory or hostile. It was a tall order, but he had taken some steps in the right direction and had seen they were steps worth taking. Even so, when given the chance, he would much rather spend time with Maggie.

"Are you hungry?" Troy asked.

"Yes. Famished," Maggie answered. "How about pizza and salad at Slice of the Moon?"

"Sounds good to me." Instead of taking the turn toward Maggie's house, Troy continued on the main road that led into town and found a place to park only a short walk from the restaurant. Slice of the Moon claimed that their old brick oven, the original oven from their first day of business in 1954, was the secret to their consistently delicious pizzas. The smell of onions, peppers, and any other topping one might wish to have baked within a seasoned sauce and melting mozzarella had an intoxicating way of warming the air and sending appetites into overdrive. Zipping their sweatshirts and pulling up their hoods, they walked arm in arm until they reached the entrance and waited to be seated.

They slid into the booth in the back corner of the restaurant near the commotion of the kitchen. It was the only open table, and they were hungry enough not to care where they sat. They were regulars at Slice of the Moon and could always agree on pizza with mushrooms, onions, peppers, and black olives along with a house salad with cheese, so they were ready to order when the waitress came to their table.

"It was so good seeing Abe today," Maggie said. "My roommates and I were at his shop a lot when we first moved into our place." She tilted her head and began twisting a strand of her hair, a habit that kicked in whenever she was thinking something through. "As a matter of fact," she smiled, "I think most everything we have in our house came from Abe's shop." She opened the cloth that covered the basket of bread the waitress had just put on their table and pulled off a piece of bread for Troy and one for herself. "He seemed to be extra generous giving us good deals 'cuz he knew we had so little money." She dug her knife into the butter in the white porcelain cup and began spreading it on her bread. "When he found out my mom was moving to Vermont to live with her boyfriend and that I wanted to stay here to finish school, he made a point to make sure I had what I needed, including lots of encouragement."

"What was your mom thinking you would do when she moved to Vermont?" Troy asked.

"I guess she just assumed I'd want to go with her." Maggie took a bite of bread. "Anyway, I'm glad I stayed. I know it'll take me a long time to finish school at this rate, but I'm not in a hurry." She smiled at Troy. "Besides, if I'd gone to Vermont, I wouldn't have met you."

Troy raised his water glass as if making a toast, "Here's to the good luck that happens when we least expect it."

Even those who wish to find happiness
and overcome misery
Will wander with no aim nor meaning
If they do not comprehend the secret of the mind
The paramount significance of Dharma.

This being so,
I shall hold and guard my mind well.
Without the discipline of guarding the mind,
What use are many other disciplines?
V. 17, 18

Abe had asked Troy to meet him at the shop by six-thirty Wednesday morning. Troy was used to dragging himself out of bed before dawn in order to set up for breakfast at the diner. And after meeting Grace, he had begun setting his alarm a little earlier so he could practice the meditation she had taught him. There were some days when the lure of sleep was more powerful than his ambition to meditate, but as time went on those days had grown fewer and farther between. He had noticed that the day went more smoothly if he had taken the time to sit and simply follow his breath the way Grace had shown him. "Even ten minutes on your cushion is better than no minutes," she had explained. He didn't have a cushion, but he folded a blanket and put it on the floor in his bedroom. In time he found that the quiet stillness of the morning was a touchstone he could draw strength from like the wisdom of a sacred elder. He made sure he sat in that stillness before he left for Abe's.

⌒

When Troy pulled into the parking lot, Abe was already outside, checking the truck to be sure all the dollies, hand trucks, and moving pads were loaded.

How the Root of Kindness Works

"Good morning." Abe's smile was as welcoming as his voice. "We've got a perfect day. No rain, no snow, and a nice cool breeze." He closed the two back doors of the van where Olde and Older was advertised in black and gold lettering.

Troy walked across the parking lot, the sand and gravel crunching under his work boots practically echoing in the early morning air. "Good morning, Abe," he answered. "Yeah, it's a perfect day for sure. There were patches of fog coming up along the river, but it's already burning off."

"Come on inside," Abe said. "I've still got a few odds and ends to wrap up." He led the way past tables, sofas, and lamps. Troy noticed that some of the pieces in Abe's store were elegant and looked like things he had seen in decorator magazines Maureen kept on the coffee tables at home. Others were quite ordinary and roughly worn as if they had survived life in one of his friends' apartments. Abe turned a corner behind some tall shelves, and Troy followed him through a doorway and up a flight of stairs. Halfway up the staircase, a small window was cranked open. A jade plant in a red cloisonné pot sat on the windowsill soaking in the first rays of the morning sun. Another doorway at the top of the stairs brought them into the second floor apartment where Abe lived and also kept his office. The musty smell of the shop was replaced by something sweet and smoky that reminded Troy of a blend of wood smoke and pipe tobacco.

"Have a seat." Abe moved some books off the cushion of the rattan chair for Troy and added them to the pile of books on the end table.

Troy pointed to the old black telephone that sat on Abe's desk. It had a dial and a loosely coiled cord that looped around the base of the phone.

"Does that thing really work?" he asked.

"You bet," Abe replied. "It works as well as it did when I got it over forty years ago. I have a portable phone with an answering machine in the kitchen." He talked while he looked through papers on his desk. "I've had to replace it several times. The new phones don't hold a candle to this one here."

"I guess not." Troy laughed. On the wall, a black and white photo of a group of soldiers gathered around a tank caught his attention. Some of the men wore helmets; all were in fatigues and boots that laced up just below their shins. One of the men was wearing sunglasses and had a cigarette hanging from his mouth. His posture and smile were loaded with the cockiness only a young man dares to have. The mountains, clusters of trees, streaks of clouds, and some thatched huts in the background were like a watercolor in shades of grey in which the harsh machinery of the tank and the weapons didn't belong. Troy was about to look more closely to see if he might be able to recognize Abe in the picture when Abe handed him a spiral bound book of maps and a metal tool box. "Here, take these out to the van, please. I'm going to grab some sandwiches, and I'll meet you out there."

Walking toward the apartment door, Troy's view was opened to a large room that had a fireplace built into the far wall. Over the mantel was a mirror framed by a carved ebony border of tiny squares. On each side of the fireplace were tall porcelain vases the color of butterscotch. Bands of black enamel, painted with vines of delicate flowers, surrounded a phoenix taking flight in the center of each vase. Partially drawn bamboo blinds filtered the morning sun and washed the pine floor with dark honey light, illuminating the gold painted statue of a Buddha sitting prayerfully on an oak table. Troy would have liked to go further down the hallway to see more of the apartment, but he was there to do a job and it would have been presumptuous to walk, uninvited, through Abe's home. So he opened the door and retraced his steps down the staircase, through the shop, and back outside.

> *"I am ever dwelling in the presence*
> *Of all the Buddhas and Bodhisattvas*
> *Who are always endowed*
> *With unobstructed vision."*
>
> *By thinking in this way,*
> *I shall mindfully develop a sense of shame,*
> *respect, and fear.*
> *Also through doing this,*
> *Recollection of the Buddha will repeatedly occur.*
> *V. 31, 32*

Troy opened the passenger door of the truck and sat, waiting for Abe, with the book of maps on his lap and the toolbox on the floor between his feet. He watched a flock of blackbirds fly like a fast moving cloud to land on the branches of a maple tree.

Abe walked outside wearing a flannel jacket and carrying a small cooler. "We've got about a forty-five minute drive. Are you hungry?"

"No thanks. Not yet," Troy answered.

Abe put the cooler behind his seat and climbed into the truck. "Could you pass me the maps?" he asked. "I want to find back roads to avoid traffic."

Troy passed the book of maps to Abe. The page corners were softened and curled from years of use. He didn't know anyone who used maps anymore. He and his friends found their way places with a GPS, listening to robotic voices with strange accents calling out street names and directing turns and lane changes.

Abe opened the book to the map he wanted and handed it back to Troy. "This is where we are," he said, pointing his index finger on the page. "And this is where we're going." He drew his finger along the roads on the map until he landed at their destination. "I'll just need your help when we get to this area." He emphatically tapped a spot on the page.

"Okay. No problem." Troy tried to sound more confident than he felt. He didn't want to admit that he had never worked well with maps or that he relied on a GPS to get around.

Abe backed out of the parking lot and turned onto the road that Troy had traveled in on. The river flowed like liquid silver under the powder blue sky, and the pink blush that glowed on the horizon was the day's last trace of sunrise. Purple-grey clouds stretched for miles like a chain of islands dotting the sky.

"Maggie told me you're really quite something on the guitar," Abe said.

"Well, that's because she doesn't play, and she's easily impressed."

"Or," Abe proposed, "maybe it's true for her and that's all that matters."

"I'm practicing a lot and am taking some lessons—trying to learn the stuff I need to know so I can get into the music program at school." Troy was watching street signs and checking the map while they drove. "I want to take some business classes too."

"It never hurts to have options," Abe offered.

The business classes were the conditions Troy's father demanded in exchange for having his financial support. Troy resented that he was in no position to refuse his help or his demands. So he worked hard to convince his father that if he could take music classes too, he would combine music and business together into something lucrative. He needed to follow through with his promise to work much harder in his classes and feared that his allotment for second chances might be running low. It wasn't that he wasn't willing to

How the Root of Kindness Works

work hard; he just didn't have a good track record where schoolwork was concerned.

"Before I came back home, I was at a college in New Hampshire. I made some bad choices and didn't handle some problems very well, so I blew a lot of options then." Troy looked out the window and watched a pair of ducks come in for a landing on the river. It was still uncomfortable for him to think about all the time he had wasted drinking and doing things he wished he could undo. "I'm trying to make up for that now."

"I think you'd have to look pretty hard to find someone who doesn't have at least a few regrets for things they've said or done, or decisions they've made along the way. The key is doing exactly what you're doing—recognizing what doesn't work and fixing it." Abe glanced over at the map Troy was holding. "We're about to pass Orchard Street. Do you see where we are?"

"Yeah, I do." Troy looked down the road as they drove past it. "I don't see any orchards though."

Abe laughed. "That's because they plowed them all down to build the road. When I was a kid, there was an orchard here filled with all kinds of fruit trees. My brothers and I used to work in the summers helping old Mr. Jamieson pick pears, peaches, and, at the end of the summer, apples. He'd pay us by the basket so we wouldn't waste time throwin' 'em at each other." He shook his head. "No one worried about child labor then. We'd only get about ten cents per basket, but we were in heaven, climbing trees and eating the most delicious peaches this planet's ever grown."

Abe's silver hair looked like fine spun glass in the sunlight, and Troy tried to picture him as a young boy, spending his summers climbing trees with his brothers. All that came to mind were images of *The Little Rascals* TV series his dad had insisted he watch. Hearing his father laugh at those films was at least as funny as the films themselves.

They drove along in silence, each floating their memories on the river's current. Troy's amusement in *The Little Rascals* moment began to fade into the familiar confusion that had interrupted and redirected all that he had understood as safe and good. Sitting on the couch with his father, laughing at *The Little Rascals*, he had no inkling that his dad was about to leave their family to start a new one with Maureen—a woman who hated everything about his father's past, most especially Troy. This was an emotional place Grace had shown him he had the freedom to leave, and looking forward instead of looking back was helping. He returned his attention to the task of watching the map and the road they were traveling.

"When I was leaving your apartment," Troy remarked, "I saw you have a Buddha statue." Thinking about the day he found a book on Buddhism in Grace's bookshelf that had piqued his curiosity, he continued, "I've been learning about Buddhism recently. Where did you find the statue?"

"Well, it's a bit of a story." Abe took his eyes off the road just long enough to glance at Troy. "Are you sure you want to hear it?"

"Absolutely sure," Troy replied.

"Well, true beginnings can be vague, but since I saw you checking out the photo on my office wall, I think I have to start there." Abe slowed down to read a street sign before he continued on. "Those guys you were looking at were my best buddies when I served in Vietnam." He paused and sighed, sending a horsefly that had perched on the steering wheel back into flight. "Only two guys came home alive—Pineapple and me. His real name was Jimmy, but he was from Hawaii so we called him Pineapple." The pieces came slowly. Abe needed to hold each piece of the story in front of his mind to look it over before the words could come.

"Pineapple died about ten years ago. His liver couldn't handle the alcohol he poured through his body. But his heart and mind couldn't handle the memories of Nam, so he drank. In a way, Pineapple died on the battlefield like the other guys." He cleared his throat before he went on. "I'm getting sidetracked. Sorry." He smiled at Troy. "Another one of the guys in the picture, Eddie, was a few years older than the rest of us. He was a genuine product of what they used to call the Beat movement. Have you heard of that?"

"Um, no," Troy answered. "I mean, it sounds sorta familiar, but I don't know anything about it."

"In a nutshell," Abe explained, "it started at the end of the 1940s with a group of American writers and continued into the 60s, spreading into a much larger movement that rejected just about everything that was conventional. Those people loved to defy rules, and their literature, poetry, and jazz was an expression of that attitude. Among other things, they liked the philosophies found in Eastern religions—which brings us back to Eddie." He laughed at the oddly colorful slice of history that influenced so much yet seemed to be unknown by Troy's generation.

"Eddie was our company philosopher. At night, when it was so dark you couldn't even see your hand in front of your face, we would listen to him talk. We were desperate to have the sounds of the jungle filled with anything that could take our minds away from the nightmares of our waking life and the fears of what was hiding in the darkness around us." Abe stopped at a traffic light and signaled to turn. "Okay, we're turning onto Winfield. Do you see that on the map?"

Troy had lost track of where they were and quickly scanned the map. "Um, yeah, it's right here," he answered. "It looks like we stay on this for awhile until we get to Route 108."

"Eddie used to talk a lot about Kerouac. Jack Kerouac was one of the writers from the Beat movement. In fact, I'm pretty sure he was the guy who came up with its name. Eddie had an amazing memory for recalling passages he had read. I don't have that gift, so I'm sure I don't have this exactly right, but Eddie told us that Kerouac said something about the universe being one vast sea of compassion—a veritable holy honey beneath all this show of personality and cruelty. I liked that a lot because with death being a very real possibility on the other side of every breath I took, I hung onto that and convinced myself of its truth."

As Troy listened, he tried to imagine himself in a foxhole with Abe and his friends. He couldn't fathom being in the kind of darkness Abe described, exposed and vulnerable like a fish captive in a fisherman's net.

"Eddie had read a lot about Eastern religions and used to tell us things he knew about, like Buddhism and Taoism. One night he told us about The Four Noble Truths. By the way," Abe said, "everything is numbered in Buddhism. Just when you think you've got something down, there's another numbered list to learn about."

"That sounds like it could get complicated," Troy said.

"It seems that way at first," Abe said, "but then you grow to realize that it's just a way to help you keep track of things by keeping them structured in your mind.

"Eddie told us that the first Noble Truth is the truth of suffering, and that suffering is the basis of existence as we know it. This, by the way, is known as samsara or cyclic existence. Suffering seems like a strong word, but I guess they like that word because it covers everything from mild discontent to the most extreme and worst kinds of suffering. Since we were all witnessing the same horrors, Eddie didn't get any argument from us on that one."

How the Root of Kindness Works

Even though they had left the river behind, the road flowed with a similar fluidity of gentle curves bordered by rocks that were balanced like loose fitting puzzle pieces into stone walls. "The second Noble Truth," Abe continued, "is called the origin of suffering, which says that suffering is caused by things like desire, hatred, and ignorance. And, by the way, those causes are known as yet another list called the Three Poisons. If you ever find yourself aggrivated or unhappy, you can be sure that one of those Three Poisons—desire, hatred, or ignorance—has infiltrated your mind. Suffering caused by ignorance includes not recognizing that everything changes and that suffering itself is impermanent. You see, suffering doesn't just happen out of nowhere—there are always causes and conditions that create it." Abe looked at Troy again. "Are you still with me?" he asked.

"Yeah, I think so," Troy answered. He remembered hearing about the Three Poisons from Grace, but hearing about them in the context of the Four Noble Truths was new to him.

"Okay," Abe went on. "Then that leads us to the third Noble Truth which is the cessation of suffering. If we understand there are causes of suffering, that means we can stop its causes, and, therefore, true happiness is possible. And finally," he slowed down and softened his voice, "the fourth Noble Truth says that there is a path that will lead to the end of suffering."

Abe rolled down his window and leaned his head to feel the air and the sun on his face. "That was our last night with Eddie."

Troy felt the slamming impact of those words deep in his heart.

"The next day," Abe continued, "we were on patrol, and Eddie was killed by sniper fire." Waiting at an intersection, Abe turned his face towards the open window and squinted into the sunlight. "When a chopper came to take his body away, I cried like a baby. As I helped lift the stretcher onto the chopper, I pictured the sea of compassion he had told us about. I pictured it as real as my mind could make it. Then, I put my head next to his, whispered in his ear, and told him to go set sail on that beautiful holy honey."

None of the words that came to Troy's mind were a match for the dignity of what he wanted to express. The sounds of the road peeling along under the wheels of the truck replaced Abe's voice. "Abe, I am really sorry. I can't begin to imagine losing all my friends like you did. I lost a friend of mine a few years ago, and it was really, really awful. But you didn't even get to just hang out with your friends and comfort each other. You had to keep marching on, just hoping to survive, and hoping to get home."

"That's basically how it went," Abe said. He was quiet for a moment before he continued. "Coming home was no picnic either. My tour was over about three weeks later. In those days there was no heroes' welcome. Instead, it was entirely possible that you'd be a target for someone's rage against the war. Even though I dumped my uniform in the airport trash like many returning soldiers did to avoid being harassed by the civilians at home, vivid memories and fear followed me like a shadow in the afternoon sun."

Troy was spellbound, absorbing the piece of Abe's history he had just heard and trying to reconcile the happy, easy-going man driving the van with the young soldier who had somehow survived hell. He turned his attention back to the road just in time to see a blue and white sign. "There's Route 108." Troy looked at the map, trying to remember the route Abe had traced earlier. "What's the name of the road we're looking for?" he asked.

"Perry Street. It's off of Newport," Abe replied.

"Okay, I see it. We're good," Troy said. "I don't know how to gauge miles, but we stay on this for a stretch."

"See that thing on the bottom that looks like a piece of a ruler?" Abe reached over and pointed to the lower corner of the page.

"Yeah."

"That tells you what the measurement of distance on the map equals on the road."

Troy used his fingers to space the distance and held them to the stretch of road they were following. "I guess it's about five miles until we turn onto Newport."

Picking up the thread of his story, Abe continued, "After I got home, I found a job with a moving company. Moving furniture was easy work for me. I was strong, and the guys I worked with were an interesting collection of characters, so they kept me distracted." Abe laughed. "They also kept me entertained. Some days we laughed so hard, it's a miracle we didn't hurt ourselves." Abe's smile was back, and Troy felt the weight of Vietnam dissolve. "Laughter and all, those guys were serious about their craft. They were old-school guys who took pride in their work and viewed it as a trade to be respected. They worked together like a well-rehearsed team. They knew when to bend, which hand to grab a piece of furniture with, how to tilt a heavy piece and use their knees to straighten it just so. It was like choreography." A school bus stopped ahead of them to pick up a group of students who filed sleepily onto the bus. The hoods on their sweatshirts covered their heads like blankets in which they could continue to sleep.

"One day we got a job where an entire house had to be emptied after the owner died, and the family wasn't interested in taking anything. The man's wife had died, and he lived alone. His career had been in Indonesia back in the 1920s, so he had a lot of unusual artwork and furniture." They drove along behind the school bus, stopping at ends of driveways and street corners. "Now, keep in mind, if I wasn't working, I was at home trying to hide from everything that scared me to death. And since I couldn't escape my own mind, there was no hiding. When the other movers and I went into the house to see what was there, the first room I walked into brought me face to face with that statue you saw in my apartment. Before I knew what hit me, the last night with Eddie and the scene of the morning that followed reenacted itself like live footage in my mind. All pride was out the window as I fell apart, dropped to the floor, and sobbed. The last thing

I wanted was for those guys to see me crying, but once it started, it wouldn't stop. I cried not only for Eddie and the other guys in that photograph, but for every single being that had to so much as breathe the air of violence that had transformed that beautiful land into a living hell. I cried for myself because there was no escape. I don't know how long I was there, curled up on the floor with my arms covering my head, before the sobbing stopped and I caught my breath again. And I don't know how long those men had been gathered around me, not saying a word, before I realized they had kneeled down next to me, and I was aware of their hands resting on my back and my shoulders. Kindness comes in surprising moments through unexpected hands, and the kindness that filled the room that morning was something I'll never forget."

So if, when having found leisure such as this,
I do not attune myself to what is wholesome,
There could be no greater deception,
And there could be no greater folly.
IV. v. 23

How the Root of Kindness Works

"Well, needless to say, we eventually got back to the business of finishing the job. We loaded the truck and delivered everything to the warehouse. Now, since my boss had to figure out how to unload all this stuff, this became a problem for him and an opportunity for me." Abe smiled at Troy, clearly enjoying this part of the story much more than its beginning. "Since I didn't do much in those days between work and home, I'd saved all the money I earned except for the money I gave my folks to help them out with room and board. That night, my father told me a friend of his was selling his house and moving to Florida. He also told me he'd been saving the money I'd been paying him in a bank account so I'd have it if I ever wanted to start a business, get married, or something big like that. We figured out that I had enough money to put a down payment on his friend's house. The Buddha statue was still fresh in my memory, and I think something about knowing it was just sitting in the warehouse along with everything else we'd moved that day must've given me the idea that I could open a second-hand shop if I bought that house. I talked to my boss about my plans and worked out a deal so I could buy the pieces we'd just moved into the warehouse. Everything, except for the statue, was my start-up inventory. While the wheels were spinning for my business idea, having had such a powerful reaction when I saw that statue, I became obsessed with tracking down information to learn more about the Four Noble Truths Eddie had talked about the night before he was killed. Mostly, I remembered the bit about suffering and that there was a path out of suffering. I was still a young guy then, and the prospect of living out the rest of my life terrified, unable to sleep through horrifying nightmares waking me each and every night, was more than I could bear. I reviewed the Four Noble Truths in my mind. I knew I was suffering. I definitely knew there were causes for my suffering. And, if there was a chance that this Buddha character had figured out some way that I could break free, then I was ready to learn whatever he had to teach."

"There's Newport Street," Troy pointed ahead and to the left. "Perry should be coming up pretty quickly on our right once we're on Newport." Troy wished it would be a longer drive so he could hear Abe tell him more. He was thinking about Grace and how odd it was that he would be hearing more about Buddhist teachings now with Abe. Grace would probably tell him it had everything to do with karma.

"So that's the story of how I got the statue," Abe said as he turned the corner onto Perry Street. He pulled a slip of paper from his shirt pocket and glanced at it. "We're looking for number thirty-seven." He drove slowly while he and Troy watched the house numbers progress along the road. "Here it is. And there's the realtor waiting to let us in." Abe backed into the driveway and stopped to evaluate the front entrance to the house that had a narrow staircase. He then rolled a little further towards the back door where there was a wide porch attached to the house with only a couple of steps leading towards the driveway. He parked with the rear end of his van near the steps. "C'mon, Troy. Let's go say hello and get started."

Troy got out of the van and stretched while he waited for Abe to take a clipboard out from under the seat. Together, they walked to where the realtor stood near the for sale sign in the pathway waiting to meet them. "Good morning, Phyllis. I'd like you to meet Troy—he's helping me out while my regular guy's away."

"Good morning." Phyllis first shook Abe's hand and then Troy's. "Nice to meet you, Troy." She adjusted the strap of her purse on her shoulder and opened a folder to review paperwork with Abe. "Everything's all set for you inside. I have your agreement right here." She handed some papers to Abe and closed her folder.

Abe slipped the agreement under the papers in his clipboard. "Thanks. Now, if you'd just sign this for me...." He handed her the clipboard and a pen.

"The man who lived here was an interesting man," Phyllis said as she signed the paper for Abe and handed it back to him. "I remember him from when I was a child. As a young man, he was a handsome guy with a beautiful wife and daughter. Sadly, his daughter died of a rare cancer when she was only fifteen years old. Just thinking about it still breaks my heart. As you can imagine, it was a devastating loss. About five years later his wife died. Everyone in town knew it had to have been the grief that took her life. So this poor man was alone. What a kind and gentle man he was—I still remember how tenderly he cared for his daughter. He'd bundle her in a warm blanket on days like today and push her in a wheelchair to take her on long walks through the neighborhood. They'd stop along the way to admire the flowers beginning to bloom or to greet neighbors. He set up bird feeders in his yard so his daughter could enjoy watching the variety of birds that came around, and he taught her about their migration patterns and which seeds attract different birds." Phyllis' eyes began to water. "Oh my, I'm sorry.... I'm not being very professional, am I?"

She wiped a tear from under her eye and tried to laugh the emotion away.

"That's okay, Phyllis." Abe reassured her.

Even though they were only about a two hour drive from where Troy lived, the small town feel of Phyllis knowing so many details of this man's life felt like he'd slipped into a 1950s Norman Rockwell world.

"Anyway," Phyllis continued. "After his wife died, he became very reclusive. A rumor went around that he had inherited money from a wealthy uncle, but whether or not it's true, no one ever knew for sure. He stayed on in this house and kept to himself. He continued feeding the birds and even put bowls of milk out for the neighbors' cats. Oh, he was a good man." She shooed a fly that had been circling too close. "He was one of those guys who liked to tinker with motors, so he managed to keep his old Impala running well enough to get to the grocery store and do other errands here and there. Everyone liked him but respected his privacy. As he grew older, neighbors brought casseroles to his door. He'd always thank them politely but never said much more than 'thank you' and 'have a nice day.'" Looking at the house as if the old man might be looking through a window right back at her, she added, "Oh my, I do hope he's at peace now. It's so sad that he died so alone." She turned to Abe. "Did I tell you that he died with no will and no heirs."

"No, you didn't," Abe replied. "That happens sometimes. I guess everything he cared about was already gone, so he probably figured there was no point."

"Maybe. Well, I've kept you too long already. Here's the key." Phyllis handed Abe a brass key on a piece of white string. "When you leave, just lock up and leave the key under the mat in the back. I'll swing by to get it later."

"You got it." Abe put the key in his pocket. "Thanks, Phyllis. Good seein' you. Have a good day."

"You too." Phyllis walked down the path to the sidewalk and waved, "Bye, guys. Maybe I'll see you later if you're still here when I get back." She opened her car door. "Hope everything goes well—you have my number if you need me." She started the engine and drove away.

Abe and Troy walked up the path to the front door. Crocuses poked their first leaves through the soil, spotting the lawn that had yet to warm into the green of spring, and a chipmunk took cover under the hedges that lined the path. "Okay, let's see what we've got," Abe said as he opened the door and found a light switch in the hallway to light their view.

Having firmly seized the Awakening Mind in this way,
Conqueror's[1] Children must never waver;
Always should they exert themselves
To never stray from their practice.

IV. 1

Troy followed Abe from room to room—first downstairs and then up. Abe quietly noted everything in his mind that would be loaded into the truck. Years of practice made it possible for him to visualize how each piece would fit. "This looks pretty good," he said, taking another peek into one of the rooms. "We'll have this done by the end of the day." He led the way downstairs to the back door. "I always donate a few pieces of furniture to the charity a buddy of mine runs that provides safe shelter to victims of violence." He unlocked the back door and wedged it open with a folded piece of paper that he had found on the kitchen counter. "Rich will be here in less than an hour, so I want

---

1 A Conqueror in Buddhism is a sentient being who defeats the suffering realms of Samsara and becomes Enlightened. A Conqueror's Child is someone who has made a commitment to help all sentient beings reach that same state of Enlightenment by helping them while they are in Samsara.

to get that stuff outside for him first." He pulled his keys from his pocket and tossed them to Troy. "Can you back the truck up a ways so he can pull his truck over here?"

Troy reached to catch the keys. "Sure," he said.

Abe took off his jacket and draped it over the deck railing and watched Troy as he headed for the truck. He learned a lot about people by watching how they approach something unfamiliar.

Troy inched the truck back slowly, relying on the side mirrors as a guide. He wasn't used to driving a truck that size, and the clutch pedal took some getting used to. He set the brake and closed the door, startling the robin that a cat had been stalking from behind a weathered picnic table.

Abe laughed. "You saved a bird but you just ruined the cat's day!" He walked onto the lawn, crouched down and extended his finger, brushing it across the short blades of yellow-brown grass. The cat remained sphinx-like under the cold shade of the picnic table. Squinting its moss green eyes in sharp focus on Abe's finger with typical cat indifference, it did not budge. Abe laughed again and then groaned with his effort to stand. "Okay," he said, "let's get this show on the road. We'll start with the bedroom upstairs—the one with the twin beds in it."

They took the bed frames apart and carried them outside. A bookcase, a small bureau, a chair, a couple of lamps, and a painting of two horses drinking from a stream were all carried onto the deck. Troy wasn't sure how Rich's charity worked, but he figured this furniture would begin a new home for someone or maybe for a family with children.

Abe held the painting for Troy to see. "Does this seem like a peaceful image to you?"

Troy tried to imagine what it might be like to see the painting through the eyes of a frightened child. Yellow-leaved aspens framed the sides of the painting, and a grey-blue range of mountains filled the background. "Yeah, the horses look kinda protected by their environment." He leaned a little closer toward the painting. "You can almost feel the coolness of that water they're drinking and the breeze that's moving the light on those yellow leaves."

Abe looked pleased and set it face down on the bureau. "Let's get the kitchen table and chairs outside and then that'll be it for Rich." They eased the table out, rotating it to fit through the door, and then stacked the chairs in pairs on top of each other.

"Now we'll start breaking down the other bed frames while we're waiting for Rich to get here." Even with the carpeting and curtains still in place, the house amplified the footsteps of their boots climbing the stairs in an unsynchronized rhythm as if it knew its emptiness had already begun.

Feeling uncomfortably as if his job was something like a house mortician, Troy asked, "Do you only get stuff from houses where someone has died?"

"Oh, no, not at all. Some people want to sell stuff because they need money. Sometimes people just want to move on and are ready to lighten their loads. It's a funny thing about people. When they're young, they want big houses and big yards. They pour all their money, time, and energy into filling their houses and making their yards look picture perfect. Then, as they get older, some people realize what a colossal burden they've created for themselves, and they just want the reverse of what they'd strived for when they were younger."

Troy wondered if his father and Maureen would ever realize something like that. Their house was large, and there was always at least one room in the midst of a decorating project. Shopping was practically a religious experience for Maureen, and driving a circuit of her favorite stores was her daily pilgrimage.

Abe and Troy split off into different rooms, taking beds apart, wrapping drawers shut, and padding mirrors until Rich's pickup truck pulled into the driveway, rattling the windows as it idled behind the house.

"C'mon, Troy." Abe poked his head into the room where Troy was working. "Rich is here, let's go give him a hand."

Rich and Abe greeted each other with the sort of handshakes that evolve into manly hugs punctuated with slaps on the back and laughter. Abe introduced Troy to Rich, and then the three of them loaded up the pieces, tied them securely into the bed of the pick-up truck, and sent Rich on his way. While Abe watched the truck until it was out of sight, Troy was watching Abe. He wasn't sure, but it looked as if he might be giving some sort of silent benediction that would travel with the furniture to whoever was at its destination.

⌒

I should undertake whatever deed I have intended to do,
And think of doing nothing other than it.
With my mind applied to that task,
I should set about for the time being to accomplish it.
V. 43

Abe and Troy then began the work of moving everything out of the house, wrapping some of the pieces in moving pads, and carefully loading the truck first with heavier pieces to build a base and then the smaller things on top. Conversation was reduced to Abe's instructions; there was a right way and a wrong way to do the job without causing damage and without getting hurt. Troy felt the responsibility of having Abe's life in his hands as they worked together to bring a heavy dresser down the staircase. The muscles in his thighs squirmed under the weight of gravity pulling against him, and his arms rediscovered muscles he hadn't used in years. Abe was right—it was harder work than he had expected, and he thought that after the job was done, he might actually feel that he had earned the value of the Les Paul guitar waiting for him back at Abe's shop.

"I don't know about you," Abe said, "but I'm hungry. How about some lunch?"

"Good idea," Troy said, relieved to have a chance to take a break. "Thanks for bringing it. I should've thought about that myself."

Abe set the cooler down on the picnic table and then leaned his weight on the bench to test its strength before he sat on it. "Don't worry about it. I always bring food for the people working with me. It's not practical trying to find places to buy a meal when we're on a job. This is hard physical work, and I want to make sure that the people working with me are well fed."

"Thanks, Abe." Troy watched Abe take bags and containers from the cooler and then picked up the thread of conversation from where his thoughts hadn't stopped running since their drive up from the shop. "So, Abe," he began, "after you decided you wanted to learn what the Buddha taught, how did you go about tracking down information? I mean, you don't live in a big city, and there was no internet back then."

There wasn't a cloud in the sky, and Abe scanned its wide-open blueness before he answered. It wouldn't be much longer until some elusive moment when no one was watching that the tightly wrapped buds on the trees would open into leaves. "I think of wisdom and knowledge like an infinite cosmic reservoir." He looked directly at Troy. "It's when there's a thirst for understanding that a seeker will find its source." Abe handed Troy a sandwich in a bag. "I know it's hard for you to imagine how anyone or anything functioned without the internet, but just consider that one way or another information has been passed around through-out time." He pulled a carton of iced tea from the cooler and poured it into paper cups. "The baby boom delivered seventy million teenagers into the 1960s. It was a pretty wild time when young people were hungry for new ideas, and a powerful movement existed to share them. It was as if some sleeping time capsule had awakened and opened like a giant milk-weed pod filled with seeds that burst throughout an entire generation, bringing revolutionary ways of thinking and cultural change." He arranged some carrot and celery sticks on a paper plate and placed them in the center of the table next to a can of nuts. "The way these ideas gained momentum was through things like underground newspapers, movies, college campuses and—of course—music. Music was a major vehicle for spreading ideas, protesting the war, and challenging established ways of thinking.

"The Peace Corps was new, and some young people volunteered in places like India and Burma where they were exposed to meditation and other spiritual teachings. They brought what they learned back to the West. Just like anything else with the right audience, even in its primitive and often not-so-authentic form, some of what these kids brought back home began to percolate within the younger culture. Then, those who were more serious about learning traveled to the East

How the Root of Kindness Works

to find authentic teachers and immerse themselves in study." Abe munched on a carrot while he pulled his sandwich from its bag. Watching an ant crawl at the end of the table, he broke off a small piece of bread and put it down next to the ant. "In 1959, ten years after the Chinese invaded Tibet, His Holiness the Dalai Lama and many other great Buddhist lamas fled to India. One of the results that came from the exodus of Tibetans seeking refuge in exile was the spread of Tibetan Buddhism into western countries through the generosity of many Tibetan teachers. And luckily for me, my teacher was one of them."

"How did you manage to find a Tibetan teacher way out here?" Troy asked.

"Well, I didn't find him *here*. When I wasn't working, I began spending time in the East Village in New York City. When Eddie used to tell us stories about things he'd done before he was drafted, some of his best stories came from his days hanging out in the Village. So, in a weird way, I was drawn there because it felt like I was keeping my connection with Eddie alive. I tried to find some of the places he used to talk about like Washington Square Park where musicians and poets would congregate every Sunday. Or in front of St. Mark's Church in-the-Bowery where everyone would go to find out what was going on in the Village at any particular time. I guess that sort of thing could be considered our version of what you kids do now on the internet. It was a friendly atmosphere, and I managed to find a few people who were studying with some very special lamas, so I learned some things from them and even got to listen to some teachings. One summer day I was hanging out in the park listening to music, and I got to talking with a guy who told me he was a student of a Tibetan Buddhist lama who had a monastery and teaching center in New Jersey. He told me that he would go to the monastery to help some of the Tibetan monks with English language. In turn, he would receive classes in Tibetan Buddhism and Tibetan langauge. He invited me to go the following weekend to hear one of the teachings taught by the monk who everyone knew as Rinpoche. When I met him, I knew I had met a being who had qualitites like no one I had ever encountered. To this day, that still holds true. Long story short—I went that weekend and continued going as often as possible from then on. That's how I became one of Rinpoche's students.

~

How the Root of Kindness Works

Although enemies such as hatred and craving
Have neither any arms nor legs,
And are neither courageous nor wise,
How have I, like a slave, been used by them?

For while they dwell within my mind
At their pleasure, they cause me harm,
Yet I patiently endure them without any anger;
But this is an inappropriate and shameful time for
patience.
IV. 28, 29

"Before I met Rinpoche, I knew the nightmares and everything else that had me in a somewhat perpetual state of terror weren't only the result of what I *witnessed* in Vietnam. It also came from what I *participated* in and the things I did in order to survive. Of course I understood the war wasn't my idea and that in war the instinct to protect yourself and your friends is hardwired into all of us. But, if ever there were a first-hand experience of descending into hell as the result of killing and hatred, I got a glimpse of that experience in a big way. Like the aftertaste of rancid food, the taste didn't go away just because I made it home and threw my uniform away." He held the can of nuts out for

Troy to take some and then poured a fistful for himself. "I could still vividly hear the sound of passing bullets in my mind, and I could still feel the sensation of extreme fear as my pounding heart exploded through my chest when a grenade went off within feet of killing my buddy and me. It didn't take much—sudden noises for example—for my mind to get tricked into thinking I was right there again, fighting for my life. Away from the landscape of war, I wasn't the kind of guy to carry weapons or want to kill anyone, but if you were the unfortunate soul to startle me, you might find yourself jacked up pretty fast, looking into the raging eyes of someone who knew how to kill." Tossing the last few nuts from his hand into his mouth before he continued, "You know, I think I scared myself on those occasions more than I scared anyone else. My reactions may seem like an over-the-top example, but I came to understand that negative actions create karmic imprints that ripen into active habits, and unless they are eliminated, they grow stronger. When I met Rinpoche and began to study the dharma—that's the word for the Buddha's teachings—I learned that positive actions produce virtuous karma, and negative actions produce non-virtuous karma, and—here's the kicker—all karma is guaranteed to multiply. There was a certain logic that struck a chord with me. Everyone has a collection of both types of karma, so the overall life experience as positive or negative will tip in whatever direction is most heavily weighted. Maybe you could think of it all like a game of pool when the cue ball sends the other balls into motion. Just imagine an endless pool table with endless possibilities of balls and pockets. Then, imagine your life as the cue ball and your thoughts as the cue. You want to choose your aim skillfully and carefully, right? It occurred to me that if the negative karmic results of killing and violence could multiply with such ferocity, then what might the opposite produce? Suddenly the possibilities of that endless pool table became a lot more hopeful. Not to be overly dramatic, it was as if I discovered a rope and could climb my way out—hand over hand—from what I considered to be hell. And whenever I felt discouraged, I'd remind myself of the torment of where I'd been, and my determination would grow stronger.

"I also learned that intention has a huge impact on the result of actions. Initially, my intention was simply to feel better. I was not in a frame of mind that could take on anything more than just finding some peace for myself. If you remember the Four Noble Truths I told you about earlier, then you remember the first two state that there is suffering and then that there are causes of suffering. The third and fourth state that the causes can be stopped, and, therefore, there is a path that ends suffering. My beginning efforts were to understand what the causes were and to stop generating them. Sounds simple enough, right?"

"Yup," Troy managed to answer through the bite of sandwich he had just taken.

"Remember when I told you that Buddhists like to organize everything into numbered lists?"

"Uh huh." His mouth full, Troy muffled a reply.

"Well, positive actions and negative actions are organized into a list that's called 'The Ten Virtuous Actions,' which, just in case there's any confusion in anyone's mind, are the exact reverse of 'The Ten Non-Virtuous Actions.' They all fall within one of three categories that pertain to actions of body, speech, and mind. When I understood these lists were not demanded by someone wagging their finger at me threatening, 'you better not do this or else...' but that they were given in a compassionate way from someone who understood the laws of cause and effect—or karma—the option of being able to be proactive on my own behalf was very appealing to me. Going back to our game of pool, it was something like having a master pool player who understood the physics of the game teaching me how to align my cue and set my shots as I learned to play. So, while I was definitely mindful of what *not* to do, I began to focus my effort on the positive things I *could* do. Remember when I said that initially it was only my own peace I could think about?"

"Yeah."

"Well, it wasn't long before I understood that would come, at first only in slight glimmers, as a result of both mindful and action oriented compassion for others."

"That makes sense. So what'd you do?" Troy was listening intently to everything Abe said, and he was intrigued by how it reminded him of things Grace had taught him earlier in the winter. Grace had shown him that Maureen's hostility was a symptom of her own suffering, and, by understanding that in a very deep way, Troy could skillfully change his experience with her by replacing conflict with compassion. He found that as long as he could remember to put the things Grace had taught him into practice, things with Maureen went much more smoothly. But it wasn't always easy to remember, especially in the immediate moment of being confronted by her anger. This, Grace had explained, is why we practice mindfulness meditation—not just a little now and then, but daily—to rehearse for the moments that are loaded with potential to wreak havoc in our world. When Grace had talked to him about karma, she explained that it worked like planting seeds—she said that actions plant seeds that will grow into their similar result. Just as an apple seed grows into an apple tree, the karmic result of violence and hatred matures into an experience of more violence and more hatred, and the karmic result of love and kindness grows into an experience of more love and more kindness. She said that our present life is the result of our karmic seeds from past lives, and, depending on what we do with this life, we create the conditions for our future life. Thinking about other lives made Troy's head spin, and, even though he couldn't say without a doubt that it was impossible for there to be more lives than the one he was living, he felt more comfortable not thinking about any other life but the one he knew.

"Well," Abe said, "the non-virtuous actions of the body were pretty easy for me to stay in line with. They are: no killing, no sexual misconduct, and no stealing. Fortunately," he said with a wink, "I hadn't developed a habit of stealing or adultery, and I was always respectful of women, so I was in pretty good shape with those two. And away from war there was no risk of any more killing. But here's where the virtuous side comes into play—to protect and save life in all forms. It might seem insignificant, but I became very mindful of things like no longer absent-mindedly killing bugs *all* bugs—even the kind most people feel justified in killing like mosquitoes and spiders. Instead of killing them, it actually felt good to catch them and release them safely outdoors. It was a good way to re-channel my energy if you know what I mean. I'd seen more than enough killing already, and when I understood that protecting life is a way to mindfully plant 'karmic seeds' that will result in taking care of beings in the future instead of killing them, I was all for it. It was also around this time that I'd seen a poster for Rich's charity organization. Helping people who were victims of violence seemed like a perfect place for me to contribute whatever help I could."

Troy thought about the focused way Abe had watched Rich's truck leave earlier in the morning and how getting the painting and the other pieces chosen and set aside had been his first priority. He began to think Maggie was right and that everything Abe did had some thoughtful purpose attached to it.

Before he finished his sandwich, Abe put another tiny piece of bread on the same plank of the table where the ant was still meandering around. "You know, in hindsight, seeing that poster is just one example of how karmic seeds are ripening all the time. That poster might have been there years earlier, but without the mindfulness of my practice to protect life, I might not have had the karma to notice it even if I had crossed paths with it. It's the kind of thing that once you begin this sort of practice and experience enough uncanny stuff that happens, you begin to suspect that it's not simply 'uncanny' but completely logical and reasonable. Meeting Rich is a perfect example of that sort of result.

"So, back to our list," Abe continued. "There are the non-virtuous actions of speech, which you might think should be easy to avoid. But you'd be surprised how we can all clean up our speech if we think more carefully about the words we let leave our lips. The don'ts of speech are: lying, slandering, harsh speech, and gossiping or idle chatter." He glanced over at the cat that had assumed a regal pose on the deck railing overseeing its back-yard domain. He looked back at Troy again. "Remember the cue ball?" he asked.

"Yup, I sure do." Troy wasn't very good at pool, but he enjoyed playing the game with his friends. He knew there were some people who knew how to line their shots up like magic and could easily picture the way intention and actions could work the same way.

"Just think about how all kinds of things are sent into motion once words have been spoken. It's like the toothpaste from the tube—you just can't put it back. So, those wise words your grandmother probably told you—'if you can't say something nice, don't say anything at all'—are good words to live by.

"Finally, we have the non-virtuous actions of the mind. They are: malice, covetousness, and wrong views. I wasn't a malicious guy before serving in Vietnam, but the experience of being hated and hunted by the enemy there, and then to find out we were hated at home too—well, I'm sorry to say, malice had become part of my mental vocabulary. And, if I coveted anything, it was peace of mind. It took awhile, but I eventually learned by listening to Rinpoche and reflecting on the things he taught that it's not possible for malice and peace of mind to coexist."

When mindfulness is set with the purpose
Of guarding the doorway of the mind,
Then alertness will come about
And even that which had gone will return.

When, just as I am about (to act),
I see that my mind is tainted (with defilement),
At such a time I should remain
Unmoveable, like a piece of wood.
V. 33, 34

"Wrong view, or ignorance, can be a little harder to get our minds around. Having wrong view means not understanding how things really exist, and, because it is the cause of all the other negative actions of body, speech, and mind, it is considered to be the worst of all ten non-virtues."

"Whoa, wait a minute, Abe. Can we back up a little?" Troy interrupted. "What do you mean when you say 'if we understood how things really exist?'" He laughed to lighten his bewilderment.

"That's a good question." Abe took another sip of iced tea, then swirled the tea in his cup as he considered how he would answer. "This approaches a topic that serious students of Buddhist dharma devote their lives determined to master. It requires a lot of study and contemplation, and it gets quite involved. To understand this well, one needs to find a qualified teacher, and I would be doing you a great disservice if I gave you the impression that I could fill that role. Even if I could, there's no way I could give you the whole she-bang sitting here over lunch. But for our purposes, we can begin to get a sense of how things really exist by thinking about how they exist in dependence on other things. Nothing exists—not even you nor I—all by it-self as if it were just plopped here in an already as-sembled form. Everything exists dependent on some-thing. One of those 'somethings' we call *causes and conditions*—or *karma*. Like a tree from a seed, right?"

"Yeah, I understand karma being like seeds," Troy replied.

Okay, then look at that oak tree over there." Abe pointed to the far end of the yard. "It might drop its acorns all over this lawn, but only if an acorn survives all the hungry squirrels and meets all the right condi-tions—like just the right amount of moisture, sunlight, and the right kind of soil—will something like this magnificent oak grow."

"I haven't ever thought about karma playing a part in how things exist. But are you saying that karma is a cause?"

"Um, yeah," Abe answered. "You can think about how karma is both a cause and a result. Like how acorns are both a cause and result of oak trees." He took some more nuts from the can and popped one in his mouth.

"Things also exist in a more subtle way in dependence on the mind. The mind sees or perceives and then comes up with its concept about what an object is." Abe waited for the words to settle. "So, just hold that thought for a moment and then consider that the mind is not a physical thing. It is clear and formless, and things are *supposed* to appear to us correctly. But as a result of our karma, we have strong imprints—or habitual ways of perceiving. These karmic imprints, collected over lifetimes since beginingless time, are left on the mind the way tea will stain the inside of a teacup. As a result of karmic imprints, we have very strong tendencies to view ourselves and other things as unchanging, independently existing things. This is ignorance—or wrong view. An example that's often used to illustrate how the mind perceives incorrectly is to think how easy it would be for someone to mistake a coiled piece of rope in a dimly lit shed for a snake. The person seeing the rope might freak out and run away, or if he had a weapon in his hand he might try to kill the rope he mistakenly perceives to be a snake. With wrong view, we don't see things as they really are. Therefore, so many of the things we think, say, and do are totally out of whack.

"The 'so what' of this comes when we really see that all things exist in a constant state of flux. They're always changing and, therefore, impermanent. Everything exists in a perpetual state of becoming and decaying. Of course everything functions in a certain way, but not in the way we ordinarily think." Abe waited for Troy's frown to soften. "In other words, with the wisdom of *right* view, everything—including your life—is loaded with possibility."

"Wow. I love that thought, Abe." Troy smiled. The thought of life being loaded with possibility as the result of his own mind was an image he was excited to work with.

"So, can you understand why mindfulness is so incredibly important?"

"No sh... oops, sorry. I mean, yeah, it makes perfect sense. Mindfulness is really crucial 'cuz it's gonna be the driving force of all that potential and possibility, right?" Troy answered.

"You got it! So, let's get back to wrong views and actions," Abe continued. "Buddha taught that wrong views include failing to recognize that we have the capacity to do both positive things and negative things and that the positive things have a positive result and negative things have the negative result of suffering. And, when we're shown that this is how things work yet choose to ignore it, it's like refusing the good medicine to help us get better and taking poison instead. With wrong views, if we do harmful things to ourselves or to others, we don't even feel remorse because we're too clueless. Instead, we continue on our not-so-merry way, ripping ourselves and our world apart."

"I don't know, Abe," Troy said. "That seems like a lot to take on. I mean, that list sounds like a lot of rules, and if I were going through everything you were going through, I don't know if I would've had the patience to think about lists and numbers of this and that."

"I guess I didn't see them so much as rules as I did markers to light my way. But what I took most firmly to heart was simply to stop all non-virtuous actions, to actively practice doing the good stuff, and the biggest piece of all—because it's the foundation of everything else—to tame my mind."

"What do you mean? How do you *tame* a mind?"

"Well, think about it—if your mind is not alert and aware, and if it's untamed like a wild animal, it'll barrel through life like a bull in a china shop. The result of a tamed mind is peace and happiness. There are many practices for getting to that point, but before getting into any of them, first we need to learn how to tell the difference between what is positive and negative in terms of actions of body, speech, and mind. It helps if we notice our feelings and examine the true motivations behind any actions we take. If they don't pass through a screening process that ensures bringing no harm to others or to yourself, and that they contain no seeds of anger, deceit, or greed, then you just don't budge until you can clear your mind of any such negativity. Those negative seeds are more destructive than you might be able to imagine just now. Therefore, we need to thoroughly comprehend that things we experience in the present are results of previous actions, and that our actions today will create the results for our future."

Abe folded the empty paper plates to begin cleaning up. "Have you had enough to eat?"

"Yeah, plenty. Thank you." Troy finished the last of his iced tea and put the paper cup inside the brown paper bag that had held his sandwich.

Sealing the cover on the can of nuts and loading everything else back into the cooler, Abe said, "Before we get back to work, there are two thoughts I want to leave you with. They are from something called *The*

Yoga Sutra written by an extraordinary being, Master Patanjali." He waited to make sure Troy was listening closely before he continued. "Ignorance has no beginning, but it has an end. And there is a beginning but no end to knowledge."

"Okay—let me see if I got that." Troy tried to organize what Abe had just said into something he could be sure he understood. "Ignorance has no beginning, but it has an end." He paused to consider—as if it could be seen—what the end of ignorance might look like. "And then, with knowledge, there *is* a beginning but no end." He thought about how Abe had described wisdom and knowledge as an infinite cosmic reservoir just hanging out there someplace, waiting for the seeker to find its source. So, if that's the case, he wondered, how could there be a beginning unless it begins in the mind of the seeker? "Is the end of ignorance and beginning of knowledge the point where someone begins to seek knowledge and then actually starts living by what he learns?"

Abe smiled at him. "I'll let you think about that and see what you come up with. But before you do, let me give you the other thought. It's a wonderful piece of Master Patanjali's advice that goes something like this: 'When breathing, empty your lungs; when learning, empty your mind; when loving, empty your heart;

and when worshiping, empty your soul.'" The sunlight danced in Abe's eyes as if they themselves were part of the sky. Abe laughed and swung his leg over the picnic bench to stand. "Now, put that in your pipe and smoke it, and let's get back to work. It's getting late."

The cat jumped from the deck railing into the pachysandra, and, without making a sound, padded her way around the corner of the house. Troy lifted the cooler from the table and walked over to the truck to put it away, repeating Master Patanjali's words over again in his mind.

⌣

Although today I am healthy,
Well-nourished and unafflicted,
Life is momentary and deceptive;
The body is like an object on loan for but a minute.
IV. 16

"We have a few more big pieces to take out, so I want to get them out first, and then we'll take care of the smaller things. If we do it right, we'll have everything packed with just enough space to roll up those rugs and slide them into the truck."

With the afternoon shadows beginning to lengthen, there was a push to work steadily in order to finish before the end of the day. An armoire, a few dressers, several bookcases, and, finally, the dining room table was the last big piece to carry. Abe climbed into the truck while Troy lifted and held it so Abe could back it into the truck, and then hopped in with him to position it.

"Okay, Troy." Abe pulled the bandana from his hip pocket and wiped his forehead. "The rest of the pieces are light. You bring 'em out, and I'll load 'em."

"You got it." Troy tried to sound more energetic than he felt. Every muscle in his body felt the aching reminder that his athletic high school days were long forgotten. He took advantage of all the lifting, carrying, and climbing up and down stairs to test how it felt to empty his lungs between each breath and noticed that it helped him use his strength in a more fluid, less stressful way. If he could empty his mind in order to learn, he wondered, would it bring a similar result?

He tried to imagine what it might be like to learn in the classes he was taking without all the resistance his mind had constructed throughout his years struggling through school—beginning with the challenge of sitting still while grade school teachers droned on and on with their annoyingly loud, sing-song voices. Even the mere flash of those memories was so uncomfortable that he had no doubt that resistance existed like a solid fortress in his mind.

More like a cry for help than a question, he heard his own voice as if someone else had decided to speak for him, "Abe, once someone's already done so much that's wrong—I mean, think how many angry words have been said, how many bugs have been swatted and killed, or, for some people, how many truly awful things they've done—just thinking about all the non-virtuous things you listed off that we're not supposed to do—how the hell does anyone even stand a chance to clean up their act enough to make a difference either in this life or for a future life?" He thought of the times when he used to drink and anger had gotten the best of him. He closed that chapter in his life, but he still carried dark regrets.

"That's the beauty of this life we have. As human beings, we have intelligence that can be put to good use, so we have the opportunity to clean up a lot for ourselves and to actually begin to make things better for others too if we don't waste our time doing senseless things." Abe gauged the shadows on the lawn. "But we've got to finish this job. We'll talk more about that on the ride home, okay?"

"Sounds good. Thanks."

Troy went in and out of the house, working from one room to the next, and carrying as much as he could manage with each trip to the truck. He began making promises to himself that he hoped he could keep, starting with getting into shape and not taking his health or his life for granted. He thought about how much he loved Maggie, and when he visualized emptying his heart, he wondered if it had only been his imagination or if he had actually felt his heart expand. His mind began to jump to all corners of his life—events from the past and hopes for the future—until he stumbled on a wire hanging from a lamp he was carrying and nearly lost his balance. *This is what Abe means about an untamed mind being like a bull in a china shop*, he thought, reminding himself to pay attention to what he was doing as he took the last few pieces from the house.

"That's it, Abe. All that's left are the rugs," Troy announced as he handed things to Abe. "Is any of that iced tea left?"

"There sure is. It's in the cooler. Would you pour some for me too?" Abe climbed out of the truck and stepped back to look it over. "I know it's weird," he laughed, "but I get so much satisfaction out of a per-

How the Root of Kindness Works

fectly packed truck! There's where we'll put the rugs."
He pointed to the spaces he'd left open as Troy handed
him a cup of iced tea. "Once we get them in we'll be
on our way." He planted a solid pat of appreciation on
Troy's back. "Thank you for all your help. It would've
been impossible without you."

Troy was caught off guard. To be the one receiv-
ing thanks felt like he was on the wrong end of the
equation. "Working with you doesn't feel like work
at all. Les Paul guitar or not, I would be honored to
help you anytime." He lightly kicked at some pieces
of gravel that were on the asphalt. "Seriously, Abe. I
mean that."

Abe leaned his hand on Troy's shoulder. "We'll see
if you still feel that way tomorrow after we unload the
truck back at the shop!"

～

When beholding someone with my eyes,
Thinking, "I shall fully awaken
Through depending upon this being,"
I should look at that person with love and an open heart.
V. 80

In the living room, a tapestry style navy-blue and maroon rug covered a large section of the floor. Its weave had worn thin in spots, and its colors faded from the years of sunlight streaming through the windows. Abe knelt down in front of one corner of the rug and told Troy to do the same at the other corner. "Okay, we want to roll evenly so the edges stay in line by the time we get to the other end." They followed the rug on their knees as they rolled it turn by turn.

It could have been either panic or excitement that made Troy's voice crack. "What the hell is that…?" Both men stopped what they were doing. Troy had sprung from his end of the rug to pick up one of several stacks of bills wrapped inside white bands of paper. He fanned the bills. "Abe, these are all one hundred dollar bills." He began picking up the other stacks counting them, "One, two, three, four, five…. My God, Abe! How much money is in here?" He counted the bills within one of the bands. "Abe, if they're all the same, then each of these is a thousand dollars."

Abe hadn't moved from his end of the rug but placed his hands more firmly on the roll to keep it in place before Troy began tugging to tear the rug like a bed sheet from the floor. Abe didn't say a word, but he watched Troy with the same intensity as he had when he told him to put his cell phone away and to memorize his phone number. When Troy wasn't able to lift the rug, Abe's hold on it caught his attention. Their eyes met, and Abe said, "Just set the money on the floor, Troy, and let's finish rolling the rug to get it out of the way."

Troy put the money in a pile near the wall. He remembered Maggie's words of caution advising him not to mess with Abe. He quietly returned to kneel at his end of the rug.

"Okay, Troy," Abe said. "I know it's hard, but I want you to try looking at those little stacks of money and view them with no more significance than any of the dressers or lamps we've moved out of here today." He began to lighten his hold on the rug. "And, if we uncover more, we'll simply move them out of the way as if they were random scraps of paper until we finish rolling and taping the rug."

Troy began rolling his end to keep pace with Abe. Short stacks of bills were in tidy rows of eight under each turn and Abe and Troy lined the floor with small heaps of money.

"What are you gonna do with all this money, Abe?"

"What do you think I should do with it?" Abe turned the question right back to Troy.

"Well, you bought *everything* that was left in the house, right?"

"Right."

"And in all those papers you and Phyllis signed was there anything in there that said what to do if you came across unexpected things like cash?"

"No."

"Then the money's yours!"

They finished rolling up the rug, and Troy held it steady while Abe wrapped tape around it to keep it tightly wrapped.

"But you still haven't told me what you think I should do with it."

"Well, you should keep it! It's yours. It's not stealing."

"And do what with it? Should I go on a cruise? Remodel my bathroom or my kitchen? Or maybe buy some new clothes?"

"I don't know. Aren't there things you need or that you've always wanted to do? If I had money, I'd buy new amplifiers and guitars and set up a studio where my friends and I could get together and jam and maybe even start recording."

"So, let's say I buy some new clothes and go on a cruise, and you set up studio space and start jamming with your friends. Will that deliver any kind of lasting happiness? Will we make anyone else's life happier?" Abe didn't really expect an answer—he just wanted Troy to question everything. "Think about the endless pool table and the endless pockets. How do we want to set up our shot?"

"Oh." Troy looked at the piles of money on the floor. Grace had explained that we can never truly be at peace—or happy—as long as there are others who are suffering. And when Abe had said earlier that his own experience of peace came as a result of compassion for others, Troy understood what he meant. The winter day when Troy handed a bag of hot food to the homeless man, he felt a sensation that could only be described as a feeling of love opening in his heart. He knew it was a small gesture, but it felt huge when he looked into the man's eyes and felt an intangible yet powerful exchange between them. "So this must be one of those times when we're supposed to think about our choices in terms of positive or negative actions."

"Well, there's nothing innately negative—or positive—about money. Remember the story about the rope that's mistaken for a snake and the craziness that ensues from that? So, how you respond to and feel about money is dependent on how your mind perceives it, right? But you're correct, there would be no stealing involved if we were to pocket that money. However, we need to ask ourselves, 'what about our motivations and intentions?'" Abe leaned the rug against the wall and began picking up the stacks of money. "If we put our motivations through the screening process we talked about earlier, would they pass?" Not waiting for Troy, he began answering his own line of questioning, "Well, maybe there's no malice involved, or covetousness, but let's look more closely at ignorance." He collected all the money into six fairly tall stacks. "Ignorance is believing that all things, objects, other beings, and ourselves exist *independent* of causes and conditions, and of one another. This is what we were talking about over lunch—the wrong view that perceives things as 'inherently self existent.' With this mistaken view, we cling determinedly to ourselves and push away the things we want to avoid. Everything we perceive and everything we do is all about ourselves—which is why we're a bottomless pit when it comes to either chasing things down or trying to avoid things in order to be happy. Ignorance also forgets that the nature of all things is to change. This changing nature applies equally to the things you desire and to the things you want to avoid. It applies to anything and everything that you believe will bring you happiness. Let's take a new car for example. The happiness you feel the first day you drive it—enjoying the pleasure of how it handles the road or the power of its engine—will, on some other day, turn to agitation when the car breaks down or anger when it's damaged in an accident. But, with wisdom, we realize that all that clinging with the wrong belief that everything inherently exists will, time after time, result in unhappiness, or the suffering of samsara—the endless cycle of existence and rebirth—like we were talking about a little while ago—'becoming and deya-ing.' Ending all that nonsense by understanding how things really exist is what leads to enlightenment—the point where perfect wisdom and perfect compassion reach balance.

"So all of this is *why* things can change and *why* the laws of karma always work. If we know this, then everything we do is infused with wisdom, creating the framework for the tenth virtuous action, 'right view.'"

With the job practically finished, Abe wanted to keep it moving. "So, yes, you're right. This is one of those times we ought to think about our choices in terms of positive and negative actions—to think of karma and how things exist. And by the way, ideally we strive to be mindful of this at all times. Now, let's get the other rugs while we talk."

"Abe, we shouldn't leave that money just lying there like that," Troy said.

"What do you think it's gonna do? Get up and walk away?" Abe laughed and led the way to the next room.

"Do you think this guy stashed money under all the rugs?" Troy asked.

"We'll find out," Abe answered. "But now what I want to know is how you might answer your question about what marks the end of ignorance and the beginning of knowledge?"

They began rolling the rug, and this time there was nothing but lint and dust underneath it. Troy thought for a minute before he answered. "Yeah, I think knowledge must begin when someone not only seeks it but actually gets the experience of the knowledge being true and begins living by what he learns." Troy held the rug in place again while Abe wrapped it tightly with tape. "The knowledge must always be available though. I mean, it must be that it's just there or it wouldn't be something some people connect with and others don't. It's just something you have to have access to."

"Which brings us to another important point," Abe said. They moved on to the next room, knelt on

How the Root of Kindness Works

the floor, and rolled the last rug across the floor and wrapped it in tape. "To be born human with resources like intelligence, good health, all the food you need, freedom to live in a place where your life isn't constantly being threatened, and with time to explore ideas is an extremely fortunate birth. And, in my own experience, I think about how fortunate I was to have met Eddie—to have retained the memory of things he told us about well enough to know learning about the dharma was an avenue worth pursuing, which led to meeting Rinpoche, my teacher. What we have as a result of others who have spent their lives seeking knowledge is the chance to benefit from what they learned. So, not with a blind faith, but with step by step experience of learning, reflecting, and meditating consistently with mindfulness on the things Buddha taught, I found that I couldn't go wrong if I continued on. Basically, the dharma provides a place of refuge—a place where one can safely go to eliminate the causes of suffering. Remember a little while ago when you asked me how does anyone have a chance to clean things up where karma is concerned?"

"Yeah, of course."

"Well, life is always offering opportunities to do that once you begin to understand how things work.

We might even have one of those opportunities right now." Troy followed Abe into the kitchen where he found a paper bag under the cupboard and helped him fill it with the money. He tried to be discreet while he took a stab at calculating how much money was there.

They carried the rugs out to the truck and slid them into the openings Abe had prepared for them and tucked the bag of money behind the toolbox. They took one more walk through the house to be sure everything was in order before they locked the back door and left the key for Phyllis under the mat.

~

Whether directly or indirectly, I should not
do anything
That is not for the benefit of others.
Solely for the sake of sentient beings,
I should dedicate everything towards Awakening.
V. 101

The sun dropped out of sight, taking with it its warmth. The scent of spring saturated the earth and the thin edge of a crescent moon hung upside down in a sky deeping into shades of indigo and red. Abe put his jacket on before he climbed into the truck, and Troy pulled up his hood and buried his hands in the pockets of his sweatshirt, shivering off the chill. They were quiet, each in their own thoughts, as they drove out the driveway and wound their way through the neighborhood onto the main road. The sound of the heater and the headlights of the passing cars had a hypnotic effect that made Troy's eyes grow heavy. Rubbing his eyes, he shook himself out of the sleepiness that had begun to settle into his body. As a child, he had heard a story of someone who had driven off the road because they had fallen asleep at the wheel. From that time on, whenever he was a passenger on long drives with his family, and later with his friends, he never allowed himself to sleep. He felt it was his duty to be sure the driver stayed awake.

"Do you need help finding your way back to the shop?" Troy held the map on his lap and was reorienting himself to find where they were.

"No, once I've gotten someplace, I'm usually pretty good finding my way back," Abe said. "Thanks though."

Troy was thinking about the man who had lived in the house, and the strangeness of having his belongings —and his money—in the back of the truck. "Abe, when you told me that now we have an opportunity to clean up some of our karma, is it because of the money?"

"No," Abe said. "Not because of the money by itself... but through the power of our intention. Money's just paper. Like everything else, it does not inherently self exist. We give it its value based on a few factors, for instance, how we view it and how we use it. What kind of feelings does it bring up: greed, generosity, or jealousy? Why do we want it? What is it that we *really* want?"

"Well, I've gotta admit, I was pretty excited when I saw all that cash. I mean, that's a dream come true."

"A dream for what though?" Abe asked.

"I always thought if I had money I could do anything I want. But I think what you were trying to tell me earlier is that some of those things I always thought I wanted would end up flipping around into something that would cause me some sort of problem or disappointment."

"If someone were to steal that money right now, would you be upset?"

"Of course. If anyone tried to steal it, I'd beat the crap out of them." Troy laughed. "Sorry. I know that's one of those things I'm not supposed to do."

"It's not the money that we have to look out for so much as it is our attachment to it, Troy." Abe tried to put this in a way that didn't sound unrealistic in its expectation. "Your attachment—your belief that the money would bring you happiness, even though six hours ago you didn't even know it was there—would've caused you to lose control and start fighting over it." Abe knew this was a stretch for most people to get but persisted anyway. "What if our imaginary thief were to have stolen a piece of fruit from the cooler instead? Would you beat the crap out of him for that too?"

"No, of course not. I'd figure he was hungry and maybe didn't have mon...ey...." he stopped himself. "Ohhhh... I think I get it. My attachment to the money would've stood in the way of feeling compassion for the guy—like, maybe I don't feel at all attached to a piece of fruit, so I wouldn't have cared if he took it."

"So what is the actual object you are either attached or not attached to?"

"Huh? What do you mean?"

"Well, would it be for the money, the fruit, or for yourself that would cause you to behave aggressively over the money and passively over the fruit?" Waiting for the light to turn at an intersection, Abe watched Troy search for his answer.

"Hmm, the money, the fruit, or myself?" Troy needed to listen to himself think out loud in order to push the thoughts along. "Which *object* am I attached to? Is a *self* an object?"

"Yeah. The self is an object in this conversation. So, bottom-line—what are you attached to?" Abe restated the question as the light turned green, and he took the turn that put them back on the road that followed the river.

Working to find the answer, Troy was forging his own connection into a deeper understanding.

"I guess it's really that I'm being attached to myself." Troy was quiet for a moment. "Um, yeah." He said it again, "It's gotta be to myself." He began pulling pieces together. "As long as someone else is suffering, then without compassion, suffering will never end. And, as long as I'm attached to myself, thinking I exist—how did you describe it? 'Inherently?'"

Abe nodded. "Yes."

"Then," Troy continued, "I'm doing that thing of chasing down all the wrong desires that end up bringing me more problems."

"That's right," Abe said. "It's like we've been looking at life in a backwards sort of way, and because of that, we've done a lot of things that have worked against us. So we want to turn it around, right?"

"Right." Troy's attention drifted for a moment, thinking about Maggie. He watched the river and thought the way the light from nearby houses floated on the sunset-drenched water reminded him of some of the paintings in the art book she had shown him the other day. He wondered what she would think about this day he had spent with Abe. Then Abe's voice pulled his attention back to thinking about attachments, ignorance, and suffering.

"Well, Troy, here comes another list. It's called 'The Four Powers of Purification.'" Abe laughed. "That probably sounds like a chapter in a chemistry textbook."

"Um, that would've been one of those textbooks I barely opened," Troy admitted. "But I think you're probably right."

"Well, we've been talking about karma and how the effects of karma are inevitable, right?"

"Yeah." Having pushed his tiredness away, Troy was getting a second wind.

"The Buddha said, '*I am the owner of my karma. I inherit my karma. I am born of my karma. I am related to my karma. I live supported by my karma. Whatever karma I create, whether good or evil, that I shall inherit.'* [2] So we're talking about karma from previous lives ripening in this lifetime, and karma from this lifetime ripening in the future—possibly in this lifetime and definitely in future lifetimes. Understanding that, we realize that there are things we can't remember having done since most people can't remember past lives, but we certainly know the potential exists that we've done a lot that's on the bad list as well as a lot that's on the good list. The fact that we're born in these human lives with all our opportunities and advantages is the ripening of the good and virtuous things we've done in the past. But the deal is, once karma *ripens*, it's finished. So unless we're lucky enough to have the sort of mind that acts on the glimpse of wisdom that's always there—provided we don't block ourselves off from it—we risk wasting the opportunities of this life by letting negative things like anger, attachment, and ignorance influence the things we do, and the good karma that has already ripened is completed without being regenerated."

"Wait a second, Abe, " Troy interrupted. "Blocking off wisdom?" he asked. "I picture that like the dividing point between where ignorance has an end and knowl-

---

2   The Buddha, Anguttara Nikaya V 57 – Upajhatthana Sutta

edge has a beginning. So removing that barrier to the beginning of wisdom could be something like realizing that it would be my attachment to my*self* that would cause me to do one of those actions on the don't's list— like beating up the imaginary thief."

"I think you could say that," Abe said. "And because that reaction to someone stealing from us is easy to imagine, it's also easy to imagine that throughout time there are many, many negative karmic seeds we've planted through actions motivated by an attachment to the self. Without wisdom, we just don't get how destructive those actions really are and that their seeds will remain until they either ripen or we create the causes and conditions for them not to ripen."

"You can actually do that?"

"Yeah, that's what the Four Powers of Purification are about. Of course, we can't eliminate a negative karmic action since it's already happened, but the four powers can stop the ripening of the action's karmic result."

"Well, what are they? How do they work?" Troy had often wished he could take back the years he had spent angry at the world after his parents' divorce and the death of his good friend. He drank way too much during that time and did things that still made him cringe when he thought about them.

"The first power is called the Power of the Object. The Power of the Object is generating compassion for all sentient beings and taking refuge in The Three Jewels. The Three Jewels are made up of the Buddha as the fully enlightened teacher, the Dharma as the truth that the Buddha taught, and the Sangha as the community of his noble teachers. The Three Jewels are where we can take refuge because they will protect us and lead us safely away from danger. We don't do this as if it's some kind of magical shield, but only after studying and then careful examination and meditation on what these things mean. Ultimately, the experience of freedom from suffering will be the result of your own understanding and your own actions."

The traffic had thinned, and the road was dark except for the light from Abe's truck. Troy was looking through the window at the stars, imagining the Three Jewels floating like a constellation in space. The night was clear and loaded with stars so bright you might think you could reach up and scoop them from the sky with your hands.

"The second power," Abe went on, "is called the Power of Regret. This is not about guilt, which is a useless form of emotional torture that actually serves to create more negative karma. It's about an intelligent re-

How the Root of Kindness Works

gret that comes from understanding the consequences of negative karma.

"This kind of regret can be productive. When you have an intelligent regret, you *really* understand the nature of what you did, and if it's something that will bring harm, you feel regret deep in your heart and want to correct it. This feeling inspires the third power."

"I really like that distinction between guilt and intelligent regret." Troy was listening closely to this part. "When I'm just wallowing around feeling guilty, I'm more likely to feel so bad that I want to hide. But intelligent regret makes me want to actually do something better, like some sort of correction if I can. Or just not to repeat the same mistake of doing things I've come to regret."

"Well, if you like that," Abe said, "then I think you'll like what comes next." He shifted his posture to ease the stiffness that was settling into his back. "The third power is called the Power of Promise or the Power of Restraint. Without an honest intention to stop doing whatever the negative thing is you just regretted, you cannot purify the karma. Some things are easier to promise never to do again than others, so if it's something that is a very strong habit, it's best to make the promise to avoid that behavior for a manageable period of time—or at least to promise to make the effort to avoid it. Without sincerity and honesty, not only is this practice useless, the karma caused by lying is very harmful."

"So, you might make the promise for a day?" Troy asked.

"Yeah, or even just an hour if that's what you know you can handle," Abe replied. "The fourth power," he continued, "is called the Power of Practice. This is when you dedicate a positive action with a strong motivation to purify the negative karma. The practice could be something like making offerings, doing prostrations, reading spiritual texts, doing special meditations, reciting mantras, or doing a good deed that is solely for the benefit of others. Whatever action of body, speech, or mind you choose to do, you want to make sure that you do it with the wisdom and mindfulness of knowing how things really work. By that I mean, with the wisdom of knowing how things really exist and that nothing exists independently. And with the understanding that everything is in a constant state of impermanence. This is one of those times when you want to take your cue stick to the pool table and very carefully line up your best shot. The other side of the karma coin is that actions motivated by the wish to attain enlightenment—the wish to achieve the mind that is so clear and free of ignorance and negative karma that it is free of samsaric existence for the sake of all sentient beings—has a special quality. With the wish to attain enlightenment—not just for yourself, but for all others—the positive effect will be experienced many times without ever being depleted."

When I promised to liberate all beings,
Who dwell in the ten directions as far as
the ends of space,
From their disturbing conceptions,
I myself was not yet freed from mine.

Thus, unaware of even my own capacity,
Was it not somewhat crazy to have spoken like that?
Yet as this is so, I must never withdraw
From vanquishing my disturbing conceptions.
IV. 41, 42

Troy recognized the stretch of road they were on near Orchard Street. They would be arriving at the shop soon. Abe had given him a lot to remember. He was hoping to put these powers of purification into practice and wanted to run through them one more time. "Abe, I want to repeat those four powers to see if I've got 'em straight."

"Okay. Shoot."

"First we have the Power of the Refuge?"

"No, Power of the *Object*," Abe corrected him.

"Oh. Right. Power of the Object." Troy repeated it over again in his mind. "And next comes the Power of Regret?"

"Right." Abe coaxed him along, offering a hint, "Then what does regret inspire?"

"Um, regret inspires the Power of Promise." Troy drummed a fast rhythm on his thighs, a habit that used to annoy his teachers but helped him to concentrate. When they made him stop, they didn't realize the learning stopped too.

"And the last one?"

"Um..." Troy closed his eyes. "Wait, don't tell me..." The drumming slowed to an end. "That's the one when I take my cue and line up the shot. Um, the Power of doing something good—what's it called? I forget."

"The Power of Practice." Abe laughed. "You got the idea though—that's important. The doing something good, as you put it, is a way you can deliberately make up for the actions you regret. And don't forget the part about intention and dedication. That's what sends the most balls into the pockets."

"Okay, I think I've got it. Thanks."

Abe slowed to turn into the parking lot and maneuvered the truck into an arc to guide the back end toward the shop. "Sorry the day ran so late. You've got a long drive home. Do you want something to eat before you hit the road?" He turned off the engine that rattled and clicked before it grew silent and opened the door, eager to stretch his legs and rest.

"No, thanks. Maggie and I are going to have dinner when I get back." Troy's legs felt heavy when he climbed out of the truck—he knew they'd be hurting a lot more by morning.

Abe brought the cooler, the toolbox, and the bag of cash out of the truck. He handed the can of nuts and a bottle of water to Troy. "Here, take these for your ride home."

"Thanks, Abe."

"When you come back tomorrow," Abe said, "we'll talk about what to do with the money. In the meantime, you can reflect on everything we've talked about today, and then we'll come up with a plan."

"Abe, that's your decision to make. Whatever you decide to do, I'm right there with you." Even though Troy could appreciate all the lofty things Abe had to say about attachment, compassion, suffering, and wisdom, when push came to shove, Troy thought he wouldn't part with the money if it were in his hands. He didn't want the burden of this decision, especially with Abe looking over his shoulder. He also didn't want to admit to the ideas that had already begun running through his mind about what he could do with even just a fraction of the cash. If Abe knew Troy's true thoughts, it would be like having God watch him steal candy from a child. Troy didn't want to admit to himself that the discomfort he was feeling was caused by his wrong view and the domino effect of attachments that are the result of that view. He was facing the barrier between ignorance and wisdom like a neon exit sign glowing in a darkened theater. If a fire were burning, he would run like hell for the exit. Was this any different?

"Drink a lot of water," Abe said. "You worked hard today, and your muscles are gonna remind you just how hard you worked when you wake up in the morning. Water helps." They started to walk towards the shop. "What time can you get here tomorrow?"

"How's one thirty? I'm only working the breakfast shift tomorrow."

"That's fine. The unloading will go faster than what we had to do today." Abe planted his hand on Troy's shoulder. "Thanks again for your help. We'll get you that guitar tomorrow."

"It's been an amazing day, Abe." Troy laughed. "Some days you just don't know what's around the corner."

"We *never* know what's around the corner, Troy. That's why we make good use of where we are." Abe turned to walk to the shop. "Drive safe, and I'll see you tomorrow."

"Good night, Abe." Troy opened the water bottle and finished half of it before he reached his truck.

Troy had been longing for the sort of insights Abe was able to offer and each answer he received prompted another question. But by the time he began the drive home, he was happy to give the questioning a break and turn up the volume on the music in his truck. Bob Marley's voice singing "Is This Love" never sounded more beautiful, as it seemed to permeate the entire world while he drove along the road, following the river into town.

　　　　　　　　　　　　‿

If I agreeably honor and entrust myself (to others),
　　　They will bring me benefit and happiness,
But if I entrust myself to these disturbing conceptions,
　　In the future they will bring only misery and harm.
　　　　　　　　　　　　IV. 33

The front light was on at Maggie's house when Troy rang the bell. He could hear Maggie running down the stairs. "Troy, is that you?" she asked before opening the door.

"Hey, Mags—yeah, it's me." He stood on the front porch, tossing and catching his keys while he waited for her.

She opened the door and hugged him. "How was your day with Abe?"

"It was a great day. Abe's amazing." Troy collapsed, sprawled out on the couch. "I'm beat up though. I found out I'm in pathetic shape."

Maggie sat down next to him. "Why? What happened?"

"I'm a wimp, Maggie. Abe's gotta be at least forty years older than I am, and I was practically killing myself to keep up with him."

"I told you Abe's amazing! Don't you just love him?" she asked.

"Yeah. Seriously, Mags, I feel like I spent the day with a human Buddha or something." Troy moved to sit up. "Ouch," he winced. "I just hope I can remember everything he told me about today."

"What did he tell you?" she asked.

"A lot of stuff. And you won't believe what we found at the house we had to empty out."

"What?" Maggie moved to sit cross-legged, facing Troy on the couch.

"I'm starving." He put his arm around her and kissed her on the cheek. "Let's get something to eat. I'll tell you over dinner."

"I'm jealous," Maggie joked. "I wish I'd been with you guys."

"Don't be jealous," Troy teased back. "It's non-virtuous." He got Maggie's jacket from the hook on the wall and held it for her to put on.

"Non-virtuous?" Maggie laughed. "What the hell are you talking about?" she slid her arms into the sleeves and zipped up her coat.

"I'll tell you over dinner." Holding the door for her, he asked, "Slice of the Moon again?"

"Sure. I'll drive," she offered. "You're tired."

Maggie's car doors creaked on their hinges, and there was rust near the fender, but the engine still ran well enough for her to get to school and work. She had a tendency to drive a little fast, but she was a careful driver. It was a short ride to the restaurant, and Troy was relieved that they found a parking spot near the entrance so he didn't have far to walk.

"Mmm... it smells good." Troy's appetite was in overdrive as they walked into the restaurant and found a table.

"I think we know what we want already," Maggie told the waitress when she brought menus and water to their table. "Could we have an order of garlic bread, two house salads, and a large pizza with mushrooms, onions, peppers, and black olives?"

"Sure," she said. "Anything else to drink?"

"Not for me." Maggie looked at Troy. "Do you want anything?"

"No thanks." Troy said, remembering Abe's advice. "Just water."

"Okay," Maggie commanded, "we're here, food's on its way—so tell me about your day with Abe. What happened?"

Troy told Maggie about Eddie and Vietnam and about the day Abe found the Buddha statue and how it led to opening the shop. He told her, as best he could remember, about all the things Abe had taught him like The Four Noble Truths, the Ten Non Virtues, the Three Jewels, and The Four Powers of Purification. The details were sketchy, but the gist of most everything was there. But, when he told her the story about the man who had lost his wife and daughter, and about the money he had left under the rug, she grew very serious.

"Troy, doesn't that money belong to someone else?" she asked.

"No," Troy explained. "The guy inherited that money from his uncle, and then he died with no heirs and no will. Abe bought the contents of the house, and the money he paid will go to the state as will the money from the sale of the house." He was quiet for a moment. "That cash is just like anything else in the house…. Abe paid for everything."

"So what's Abe going to do with the money?" she asked, taking a slice of pizza from the round aluminum stand.

"It's weird, Maggie. I mean, it all made sense when I heard Abe talk about it, but now that I'm trying to explain it to you, it just seems like it might be a little out of touch, if you know what I mean."

"No, I don't know what you mean." Maggie defended Abe, "Abe has got to be the most 'in touch' person I've ever known." She had put her pizza down on her plate and sat up defensively. "I can't imagine Abe saying or doing anything that would be anything but genuine and wise." Composing herself, her voice softened, "So what's he going to do with the money, and why do you think it's weird?"

"First of all, I don't know what he's going to do with the money. Secondly, I don't mean that Abe's weird or out of touch or that anything he would *do* is out of touch. It's just that things seemed pretty obvious and clear to me while I was there talking with him about how the intention to do things for the benefit of others creates less suffering as opposed to when we're all about ourselves. And now that I'm trying to talk about it with you, I feel like maybe *I'm* out of touch. I mean, can you imagine my dad and Maureen finding a boatload of money and even entertaining the possibility of using it for something other than a decorating project or jewelry for Maureen?"

"Yeah, but, Troy," Maggie said as she relaxed into her seat again, "sorry to have to say it—I don't want to be doing anything on that non-virtuous list—but think about how miserably unhappy Maureen seems to be. I mean, it doesn't matter how much jewelry she has hanging on her; whenever I've been at your house, there seems to be some catastrophe she's freaking out about like, 'oh my God, there's a chip in the china.'"

Troy laughed. "You're right. And that illustrates Abe's point beautifully." Troy was relieved to make sense of things again. "If I feel out of touch, it's because my perception is skewed. When I'm listening to Abe and understanding that there's nothing that exists independently or... *inherently*—don't you just love that word? It sounds so deep." He smiled. "Then the logic of helping others is a no-brainer."

The basket of garlic bread was empty, and all that remained of the pizza were the edges of crust piled on the white dinner plates. "Do you want the rest of my salad?" Maggie offered, seeing that Troy had finished his own.

"Are you sure you don't want anymore?" Troy thought if someone put another pizza in front of him, he could probably finish it as well.

"No, I've had enough. Here, have mine." Maggie swapped salad plates with Troy.

"So I'm going to Abe's after work tomorrow. Do you want to come with me?" Troy asked. "Abe said it won't take as long to unload the truck as what we had to do today."

"Sure, I'd love to go. I can help you guys," she suggested. "I'll get to spend the afternoon with two of my most favorite people—you and Abe!"

"Good. Just don't tell Abe how beat up I am, okay?" Troy finished the last piece of tomato that was left on the plate.

The waitress returned to the table to refill their water glasses. Maggie and Troy were ready to leave and asked for the check.

"Let's leave a good tip," Maggie reminded Troy. "People don't realize how hard restaurant people have to work, right?"

"Right." Troy loved the way Maggie always had enough to give, no matter how little she had.

They walked, holding hands, back to the car and left for the short drive back to Maggie's house.

"I've got to study for my test tomorrow, and you look like you could fall asleep in an instant," Maggie said as they pulled in her driveway. "So say 'goodnight,' and how about I meet you back here tomorrow after your shift and we'll head up to Abe's then?"

"Sounds like a good plan to me," Troy agreed. "Good luck on your test."

"Thanks." She kissed him goodnight. "Don't fall asleep on your ride home, and I hope you don't hurt too much when you wake up tomorrow."

However, if the elephant of my mind is firmly bound
On all sides by the rope of mindfulness,
All fears will cease to exist
And all virtues will come into my hand.

The Perfect Teacher himself has shown
That, in this way, all fears
As well as all boundless miseries
Originate from the mind.
V. 3, 6

Before drifting into sleep, images of pool games, lists of virtues, and jewels flickered through Troy's mind like swirling confetti in a parade. It was a deep sleep that absorbed his entire body into the fibers of the blankets. The night was filled with dreams like fast running episodes that pulled fragments from one into another. It could have just as easily been seven minutes as seven hours until the last dream came before he woke up.

He dreamed he was climbing a steep hill on a narrow road lined with old buildings set close together. Large, white clouds spotted the perfectly blue sky like crisply ironed doilies. Mountains with snow on their highest peaks sparkled prisms of color and the only sound was the pitch-less, hollow tone of moving air. Inside one of the buildings, Troy stood in a room with doors that opened to the view of a lake. Several people were inside the room, but he didn't recognize any of them. One man, speaking a language he couldn't understand, approached him carrying a goblet that had to be assembled by twisting the bowl-like top onto the stem. He then filled it with an amber colored liquid and gave it to Troy to drink. Its taste was unfamiliar but sweet. Troy then woke to the sound of his alarm and reflexively pushed the snooze button hoping to find the dream again. But some dreams just can't be reentered once you've awakened.

He had set his alarm early enough to leave time to meditate before work. On this particular morning, he planned to meditate on the Four Powers of Purification that Abe had explained the day before.

With just about every muscle in his body aching, Troy's entire body felt bruised. Moving slowly, he showered, dressed, and then took a seat on the

How the Root of Kindness Works

folded blanket on his bedroom floor. He sat with his legs crossed, his shoulders and arms relaxed, and the back of his right hand resting in the palm of his left. He raised his thumbs, lightly touching them together at their tips to form a teardrop circle. He lowered his eyes and began by simply breathing and counting each breath's cycle of inhalation through exhalation. He counted eleven breaths this way and then imagined a light in front of him at the level of his eyebrows. Grace had told him the source of the light could be visualized in whatever way he might picture ultimate truth and love. With that light in his mind's eye, he then followed his breath, breathing a steady stream of light. Of course, his mind wandered from time to time, but he remembered that Grace had told him that is to be expected and simply to bring his attention back to his breath. A deep peace settled within him, and he was ready to review The Four Powers.

He began first by taking refuge in the Three Jewels in the way Abe had described them. Using the light he had been visualizing, it wasn't hard to conceive of the Three Jewels as something that would guide and protect him. He held the image close in his mind while he moved to thoughts of regret. He began with things like fights he had been in when he had been drinking. He thought of lies he had told—some he remembered, and more he had likely forgotten. He thought about people he had hurt, especially one guy he knocked unconscious—and, for a second, feared he might have killed. That was the last time he drank and the last time he was in a fight. He regretted the anger he felt toward his father for all the pain he had brought to their entire family, which had become the short fuse that sparked every rage he had felt since. He thought of people he had betrayed or let down by promises he had failed to keep. He remembered Abe's instruction to steer clear of guilt by having an intelligent regret that recognizes why he would never want to bring pain to anyone or plant negative karmic seeds for his future. He had no doubt about the existence of karma or of causes manifesting their similar result. Just as Abe said it would, this regret inspired the resolve to not repeat these or other negative actions.

He took Abe's caution to heart, made the promise to restrain from allowing the negative emotion of anger to develop, and then made the promise manageable by committing to only one day. He knew he could repeat this process each day if he wanted, but by setting the promise day by day, he felt less likely to unintentionally break it.

Finally, Troy thought about the power of the practice. Abe had talked about doing something with the intention to benefit all beings. He had told Troy they had an opportunity to clean up some negative karma now, but he had been mysterious about what exactly the practice might be. Sitting on his makeshift cushion, that mystery began to dissolve. *Maggie was right again*, he thought. *There is a purpose to everything Abe does.* Abe wanted Troy to come up with his own purpose for how he thought the money should be used. Troy knew Abe would offer the money for something far-reaching and perfect. By including him in the decision, Abe was giving Troy the chance to find a similar quality intention as a natural result of a true understanding, not because Abe said it should be so.

Although Troy hadn't been in combat like Abe, he had known anger and violence that had been of his own making, and he wanted to be free from the negativity that lingered like a taunting voice that wouldn't leave him alone. Troy recalled the expression on Abe's face the day before as he quietly stood and watched Rich's truck leave the house, packed with furniture and other pieces that he had specially chosen. Troy became so moved that tears filled his eyes. The depth of pain Abe carried home from Vietnam had become the inspiration for his resolve to put into practice the teachings he had first been introduced to through Eddie and then developed by studying with his teacher. Kindness had replaced grief, and compassion was the air he breathed—every act and every thought was a deliberate practice to live for the benefit of all sentient beings. There was no remaining question in Troy's mind. He would tell Abe that he wanted the money to go to Rich's charity to help fund his work to provide shelter to victims of violence.

Unruly beings are as (unlimited) as space:
They cannot possibly all be overcome.
However, if I overcome thoughts of anger alone,
This will be equivalent to vanquishing all foes.

Likewise, it is not possible for me
To restrain the external course of things;
But should I restrain this mind of mine
What would be the need to restrain all else?
V. 12, 14

How the Root of Kindness Works

The diner was busy during breakfast as it typically was on weekday mornings. Tables needed to be cleared and reset countless times, and Troy had to move quickly to make sure they were clean and ready for the next customer. Moving his body was painful, but he found that by staying in motion the pain was less than after he had been sitting for a length of time. He reminded himself to practice breathing like he had the day before, emptying his lungs fully between each breath. It helped.

The customers dwindled down to only the few who had time to linger by the time his shift ended. All employees were offered something to eat when they finished work, so Troy made a sandwich and wrapped it to take with him before he tossed his apron in the cloth hamper near the dishwasher. Saying goodbye to the cook and the others in the kitchen, he left through the back door for his truck and drove to Maggie's.

Maggie's roommates' cars were in the driveway when he arrived, so he parked on the street and limped across the lawn to her door. He could hear the girls laughing inside, drowning out the sound of the doorbell. He pounded on the door as Maggie walked by.

She saw him through the front window and opened the door to let him in.

"Hey, Mags." He handed her a red rose he had bought from the convenience store at the gas station earlier.

"Thank you, Troy. It's beautiful." She gave him a kiss, and Troy went with her to the kitchen to look for a vase.

"How'd you do on your test?" he asked.

"I think I did okay," she said. Looking through the cupboards, she found a tall glass, filled it with water, and placed the rose in it. "I'll find out soon enough." She set the rose on the windowsill where the light would reach it. "I'm psyched to see Abe though. Look, I made him some brownies." Taking a plate of brownies covered in plastic wrap from the counter, she held them for Troy to admire.

"Those look great."

"Are you ready to go?" she asked.

"Yeah, I'm ready when you are."

The roommates were upstairs and probably didn't hear Maggie yell "goodbye" as she and Troy left, closing the door behind them.

"Do you want half my sandwich?" Troy offered once they were on their way.

"What's in it?" She opened the paper wrapping before giving him a chance to answer. She was a fussy eater and didn't always like the same things Troy liked.

"Avocado, cheese, and tomato with hot sauce," he said. But she had already handed the sandwich back to him.

"No thanks, you can have it," she said. "I had something to eat when I got back from class."

Maggie held the plate of brownies on her lap and looked out the window to the river. The sky was crystal blue, and the river was filled to its banks with light. With the branches still bare from the winter, there were no leaves to shade the water. She thought about the day she and Troy had first gone to see Abe and remembered the guitar that was the inspiration for them working together. "You haven't even mentioned the guitar, Troy. You'll be taking it home today, won't you?"

"Yeah, that's what Abe said yesterday." He was probably too distracted by everything else that had happened to feel as excited as he would have expected. "I've got to pick up some new strings for it and plug it in to see how it sounds. But I know I'll love playing it."

It was just about one thirty when they arrived at the shop and saw Abe outside greeting a customer.

Maggie climbed out of the truck carrying the brownies, and Troy lumbered out trying to disguise how stiffly he was moving. He stood behind the truck and stretched his legs before he joined Maggie, who was waiting for Abe to finish with the customer.

"It must be my lucky day. Hello, Troy. And, Maggie, what a nice surprise!" Abe welcomed them each with a hug.

"I made you brownies, Abe. I know how you love chocolate." Maggie held the plate in her hands and presented it to him.

"They look delicious, thank you." Abe invited them to come inside with him to put the brownies in his apartment. They followed him up the stairs—Troy lagging behind by a few steps. When he walked through the door, he looked down the hall to see the Buddha. Maggie and Abe were already talking in the other room. Troy walked closer to the statue where a candle and a stick of incense were burning. He thought of Abe's story about how he came to have this statue and felt a wave of emotion picturing Abe as a young man, collapsed in grief, while the men he had been working with rested their hands on him in compassionate silence. Abe's journey—his path—had been

How the Root of Kindness Works

one of immense courage and determination. Troy felt the magnitude of what it must have meant for Abe and for the others to hear Eddie's voice soothing their fears with his stories during the nights filled with enemies both unseen and unknown. He felt the horror of the day when Eddie was shot. He thought of Abe—desperate, terrified, and broken—visualizing Kerouac's sea of compassion as he whispered his parting words to Eddie: *go set sail on that beautiful holy honey.* Troy wanted to see the photograph on Abe's office wall again. He wanted to see Eddie and Pineapple and remember them the way Abe remembered them—full of the promise that life could have been.

"Troy, are you coming?" Maggie called from the other room.

"Yeah, I'm right behind you," he answered. He pushed the emotion into the space that felt like a trap door opening where his heart had broken and found his way into the kitchen where Abe and Maggie were talking.

"Whadd'ya say, are you ready to unload the truck?" Abe asked. "I've already begun taking out the stuff I could handle myself. Maggie said she'll help arrange things in the shop while you and I get everything off the truck." Abe noticed the stiff way Troy was moving and added, "Without the stairs, this is the easy end of the job."

"I'll take your word for it," Troy said. "I'm ready."

They all filed out through the door and down the stairs. Abe paused to watch a spider spinning a web in the window frame near the jade plant. Troy watched him, knowing full well that there was nothing random in any of Abe's actions. He was probably offering a prayer for the spider. Abe stopped to help a customer in the shop while Troy and Maggie continued outside to the truck.

⌒

Always being motivated by great aspiration,
Or being motivated by the remedial forces,
If I work in the fields of excellence, benefit and misery[3]
Great virtues will come about.

---

3   To work in the fields of excellence, benefit and misery means to direct one's wholesome deeds towards the objects of refuge (the field of excellence), one's parents, teachers, etc. (the field of benefit), and those who are suffering (the field of misery).

Endowed with wisdom and joy,[4]
I should undertake all that I (intend to) do.
I (need) not depend upon anyone else
In any actions that I undertake.

The perfections such as generosity
Are progressively more exalted,
But for a little (morality)
I should not forsake a great (gift).
Principally, I should consider what will be
of the most benefit
For others.
V. 81, 82, 83

"What's the matter, Troy?" Maggie asked. "You seem a little low."

"No, not low at all," Troy reassured her. "Maybe just a little reflective." He pushed at the sand and gravel with the toe of his boot. "Thanks for bringing me to meet Abe." He began to feel himself getting emotional and didn't want Maggie to notice. Instead of saying anything more, he just reached to pull her into his arms

---

4   In some editions of the text 'faith' (*dad-pa*; Skt: *shraddha*) is found instead of 'joy' (*dg'-b*; Skt: *priti*).

and held her. Breathing, he emptied his lungs—loving, he emptied his heart. He felt his heart breaking not from pain, but from the wall of ignorance that was crumbling free.

Abe came outside. "Let me show you where we're going to put everything. And, Maggie, if you can help organize the space inside a little better, that would be a big help."

"I'll try," she said.

He put his hand on Troy's back. "Okay, buddy, grab that dolly over there by the wall. I've got one over by the truck already. We'll just wheel the stuff in like this," he explained, gesturing with his hands to point the direction of the path they'd take to where Maggie was clearing some space.

Abe had a rhythm he worked with, and Troy synched his own to match it. Abe was right—using the dollies made this end of the work go much faster. Maggie knew how to arrange the furniture, lamps, and other items into vignettes so they could be nicely displayed. "I think it'll look nice if we open one of the rugs here, Abe. Then I can set some of the lighter pieces on it so if anyone wants to buy it, it'll still be easy to get to."

"Good idea," Abe agreed.

They had leaned the rolled rugs against the side of the truck. Abe evaluated their sizes to see which would fit best in the area Maggie had in mind and pulled one away from the truck. Waiting for Troy to pick up the other end, he asked, "Did you come up with any ideas for what you thought we should do with the money?"

"Yeah, I did." Troy lifted the rug from the ground. "It's kinda funny because when I left yesterday, I didn't think I'd have a clue."

"Hold the rug a little higher so we don't knock anything over on our way in," Abe interrupted. "So what happened? What changed?"

"This morning I meditated on the steps you told me about in the Four Powers of Purification. I really didn't know what to expect when I began, but by the time I reached the end, I felt like everything was crystal clear."

Abe kept a jackknife in his hip pocket and used it to cut the tape they had wrapped around the rug.

"Right here, Maggie?" Abe asked before they rolled it onto the floor.

"Sure, that'll work." She moved things out of the way while Abe and Troy unrolled the rug, and Maggie began placing chairs and end tables into an arrangement that could pass for an old fashioned parlor.

When they got back to the truck, Abe said, "I want to hear what became 'crystal clear.'"

"Well," Troy began, "I thought about things I regret. Like anyone, I suppose, I have more than a few." Troy took a deep breath before he went further. "Do you remember the year I told you about when I was in school in New Hampshire and how I really messed up while I was there?"

"Yeah, I do."

"I used to drink a lot, Abe. Actually, it was more than just a lot. I was a pretty angry guy back then. My parents' divorce had been ugly, and the mess that followed was even uglier. But I think the thing that pushed me over the edge was when one of my best friends was killed. He'd been walking home one night and was hit by a speeding car." He remembered Eddie, and decided no other details were necessary. "Well, it turns out that alcohol and I are a volatile combination. Hanging out in bars, I got into a lot of fights. My fuse was short, and if I was drinking, then any excuse for a fight was a valid one in my mind. The last fight scared me to death though because I swung at a guy and hit him in the face so hard that when he went down, he hit his head on the sidewalk and fell unconscious." Troy's voice started to

How the Root of Kindness Works

break as he spoke. "Abe, I thought I killed him." He took a breath and tried to distance himself from the story again before he continued. "If I hadn't been such an idiot, I would've hugged him in gratitude when I saw him open his eyes." He warmed his hands in the pockets of his sweatshirt—bringing those memories to mind sent a chill through his body. "So I'm glad you told me not to confuse regret with guilt and that regret would inspire the resolve—or the promise—not do it again. Even though I already swore off drinking and therefore stopped getting into fights, somehow the resolve in the sequence of The Four Powers felt more potent. So when I got to the fourth power—the part about the practice—that's when things started to really move for me. The thing I found so amazing was when I remembered something you said—something about the power of lining up the cue ball and making the shot with the intention to benefit all beings. It was then that everything became crystal clear. Your friend Rich, and your practice of giving him a donation from every job, came immediately to mind. Since Rich's work is all about helping victims of violence, if that money could go to support his work, then we could dedicate it with that intention." He looked at Abe. "What do you think?"

Abe smiled. "I think you just made a masterful shot, and you might've cleared the table." He put his hand on Troy's shoulder. "And how do you feel?"

Troy kicked at the gravel again before he spoke, "I feel a little awkward saying this, but I think I need to say it anyway, and that you'll understand—I feel incredibly moved and unbelievably lucky."

"Nothing awkward about that at all, Troy," Abe reassured him. "Do you feel any luckier than if you were keeping that money?"

Troy laughed at the beautiful simplicity of all that was contained in that question, "Oh my God, there's no question at all. Absolutely I do."

"That says it all." Abe laughed. "Okay, let's finish this up, and then we'll go inside and take care of some business. There's a guitar that's waiting for you in my office. Also, I talked to Rich last night, and he's coming by later. If you and Maggie aren't busy, why don't you stay for dinner?"

"That sounds great, but let me check with Maggie." He walked to the door of the shop.

"Maggie!" Troy yelled into the shop.

"Yeah?" Maggie came to the door, holding a vase in her hand.

"Abe wants to know if we can we stay for dinner."

"We'd love to." She looked at the furniture that was still in the truck. "Looks like you're almost done."

"We're gettin' there," Troy said.

⌒

I should conceive of my body as a boat,
A mere support for coming and going,
And in order to benefit all others
Transform it into a wish-fulfilling body.
V. 70

With everything unloaded, pads folded, and dollies put away, Abe closed the doors on the truck and drove it to park behind the shop. Troy helped Maggie set the last of the pieces into the displays she had arranged.

"Okay you two, let's call it a day." Abe looked around at all the new pieces that were filling his shop. "Maggie, I can't thank you enough. Having you here to figure out where to put everything was the magic wand that makes everything look good."

She straightened a picture on the wall. "It's fun, Abe. I feel like I spent the afternoon playing with a life-sized dollhouse!"

"Come on upstairs, we'll have some tea and relax."

He started the kettle boiling, and then Abe took three mugs from the cupboard and placed a teabag inside each mug. "How do you guys take your tea? I have lemons, honey, or cream."

"Lemon and honey, right, Troy?" Maggie answered for both of them.

"Yes, thanks."

Abe sliced a lemon into wedges on a plate and placed it next to the jar of honey that was on the kitchen table. A steaming mug was set in front of each of them with a spoon and saucer.

Troy watched Maggie twirl a piece of her hair as she looked out the window, watching cars drive past and waiting for the tea to steep. He appreciated that he knew her well enough to recognize that this was a sign she had something she wanted to sort through in her mind. And, if he waited, she would eventually let him know what it was.

Abe had taken the teabag from his mug and put it on the saucer. "Excuse me." He pushed his chair from the table. "I just remembered something. I'll be right back." He left the room and returned a few minutes later carrying the brown leather case that held the Les Paul guitar. He waited for Troy to back his chair from the table to take the case onto his lap. The cobwebs and mildew had been cleaned from the case. Lifting the lid, Troy saw the guitar had been polished and given a new set of strings. He lifted it from the case and strummed the strings slowly, listening to the tone of each string.

"Abe," Troy said, "it's beautiful."

"I took it to someone a friend of mine recommended to do a few minor repairs and just got it back the other day."

Troy closed the empty case, put it on the floor, and tuned the guitar. "The action feels great under my fingers. I can't wait to hear it with my amp." He played a few riffs and chords. "This is unbelievable." He played a fast passage and ended it with a bend of the string. "Who finds a vintage Les Paul and gets the added bonus of a day with Abe?" He stopped playing and thought a little further. "Or maybe I should've said, 'who gets to spend a day with Abe and gets the added bonus of finding a vintage Les Paul?'"

"Glad you're happy with it," Abe said. He looked at the clock on the kitchen wall. "Ah, it's time to put the lasagna in the oven." He opened the refrigerator and took out the lasagna he had made in the morning.

"Can we help with something?" Maggie asked.

"Just relax and enjoy your tea. In a little while, you guys can set the table."

Troy put the guitar back in its case. "Is it okay if I put this in your office until we leave?"

"Sure, go ahead."

Troy turned on the light to look at the photograph on the wall. There were the guys Abe had told him about. And there was Abe. Troy could easily recognize him now that he had a chance to look more closely. He was a lot thinner, and his hair looked very dark—although with a black and white photograph, it's hard to know for sure about colors. But, even so, he could recognize the intensity in his eyes. There was the guy with the cocky smile, cigarette, and sunglasses. He looked like he was ready for the photographer, but the rest of the guys looked like they weren't quite ready to smile before the picture was taken. Troy went back to the kitchen and asked Abe if he would come show him which of the guys was Eddie and which one was Pineapple. Abe left the dishes he had taken from the cupboard on the counter and joined Troy in his office.

"Pineapple's the guy right here leaning his hand on my shoulder." Then, Abe moved his finger to the guy with the cigarette and the cocky smile. "And this one here with the sunglasses, that's Eddie." Slowly, he moved his hand and pointed to the others in the photograph. "Here's Sully, Jimmy, and this guy over here we called Pedro, but his real name was Peter." He laughed. "Who knows why we called him Pedro. We must've thought it fit him better for some reason."

"When you told me about Eddie," Troy said, pointing to Eddie in the picture, "I thought that might have been him. He looks like someone who could've been quoting Kerouac." Troy leaned closer to the picture to see him more clearly.

There was a knock on the door that interrupted them. Abe left to answer the door with Troy just a few steps behind him.

"Hi, Rich, come on in. You remember Troy?"

"Of course I do, Abe. That was only yesterday. I'm not that old yet, but thanks for the reminder!" Rich laughed and shook Troy's hand. "Hi, Troy, good to see you again."

They made their way into the kitchen where Maggie had begun setting the table. "And this is Maggie."

"Hi, Rich. Nice to meet you." Maggie was folding napkins that she would put on the golden yellow placemats that reminded her of weaving projects she had done in summer camp when she was a child. Silverware had been distributed to each place setting, and, from the living room, she brought an African Violet from its place near the window and set it on the table as a centerpiece. She found a glass pitcher in Abe's cupboard, filled it with water, and then filled each of the water goblets on the table. Standing back, twirling a strand of her hair, she looked the table over carefully to see if anything was missing.

"Abe, do you have any candles?"

"Yeah," Abe answered, "in the living room, there's a drawer of them in the chest near the bookcase. I think it's the middle drawer. Let me know if you need help finding them."

"Okay, thanks." She was already in the living room, which shared a doorway with the kitchen—the room where the Buddha statue sat in uninterrupted equipoise. "I found them," she announced. "Are there candle holders in here too?"

"Um, yeah." Abe thought for a moment. "Look in the next drawer down."

"Got 'em. Thanks." She chose a pair of deep blue candleholders that fit nicely with the white candles that she had found in Abe's drawer. Setting one on either side of the abundantly blooming African Violet, the colors had a nice effect. The finishing touch, she

How the Root of Kindness Works

thought, would be the dinner plates with the red and gold painted trim that, like most everything else Abe filled his home with, had been retrieved from one of the houses he emptied.

Abe put a salad on the table, a basket of bread, and then carefully took the lasagna from the oven.

~

Having in this way examined their minds for
disturbing conceptions
And for thoughts that strive for meaningless things,
The courageous (Bodhisattvas) should hold their
minds steady
Through (the application of) remedial forces.

Being very resolute and faithful,
Steady, respectful, polite,
With a sense of shame, apprehensive and peaceful,
I should strive to make others happy.
V. 54,55

"Troy," Abe said, "come with me into the office for a moment please. There's something we need to take care of before we have dinner."

"Sure," Troy said, "what is it?"

Once in the office, Abe sat at his desk and opened the drawer. "When I told you earlier that I talked to Rich last night, I didn't mention that I told him about the cash." He took a wooden box from the drawer and put it on his desk. "You see, I had already decided that I wanted the money to go to his organization, but I very much wanted you to have an opportunity to have a choice as well." He glanced at the photograph on the wall before he continued. "When you told me your experience with the Four Powers of Purification and that Rich's charity had come to your mind to give the money with the intention of benefiting others, I wanted you to join me in presenting this gift to him. You see, from my perspective, it seems you and I share some regrets of a similar nature. We also shared the experience of discovering the money, and now we can share in the dedication of this cash." He opened the box and showed Troy the money that was now arranged under a piece of white silk, stacked in rows inside the box. "In truth, the money isn't ours to give, nor does it belong to anyone. The man who lived in that house had already paid tax when he inherited it from his uncle— the court ran its announcement in the papers of the

How the Root of Kindness Works

man's death before it could liquidate the proceeds from the house and turn it over to the state. Rich's charity is a non-profit organization, which, from what I understand, means this is a tax-free donation. You and I are merely vehicles for this money to be dedicated to benefit other sentient beings. Before we present this to Rich, I would like you and I to take a moment here and now to think about our purpose in this—this 'offering,' if you will. Think of all sentient beings throughout all of existence and feel the deepest wish you can bring into your heart and your mind—for every single being throughout the entire universe to be free from the causes and conditions that create suffering, and for every single being to meet the causes and conditions that will bring happiness." Abe looked into Troy's eyes, waiting to see that the importance of properly making his dedication had been understood.

Troy's eyes moistened as he felt the relief of clearing and purifying some of the negative actions from his past, and the confidence he felt that things could only get better if he remained vigilant to the activity within his mind. He pictured the pool table Abe had talked about and mentally lined up his cue. "I'm ready," he said. He looked at the photograph on the wall before he lowered his eyes and sat in silence with Abe, each of them reviewing the Four Powers, and, finally, making their dedication.

There was something about the sound of their breathing—maybe it was the way one breath was drawn especially deeply before it was released—that cued them to meet each other's eyes. Without saying a word, they stood to carry the box into the kitchen where Rich and Maggie were serving the lasagna onto the dinner plates before setting them one by one on the table.

Seeing that the table was set and the dinner served, Abe asked Maggie and Rich to take a seat at the table. "Maggie, once again, you have made everything look beautiful. Thank you."

Abe cleared his throat, "Rich, Troy and I would like to offer the money that is in this box to be used for the purpose of enhancing and, hopefully, expanding the superb and generous work you do to provide safe shelter to victims of violence. As a Buddhist, I've learned to count fairly well, and by my count, there is $84,000 inside the box. May this offering bring peace and an end of suffering to all sentient beings."

Rich drew his hands as if in prayer toward his mouth. Unable to speak, he lowered his eyes. Abe,

Troy, and Maggie were silent as a tear inched its way down Rich's cheek. It was a long and sacred moment that no one wanted to disturb until a robin, perched in a branch outside the kitchen window, sang its aria to the dusk.

Rich was the first to speak, "Abe, Troy, 'thank you' doesn't begin to touch the depth of gratitude I feel in this moment." He paused to compose his thoughts. "Abe, I didn't tell you last night when we talked that a benefactor who has supported us for many years has donated a house with the request that we extend our help to support veterans who are coming back from their service in Iraq and Afghanistan. Many are returning limbless, homeless, and with emotional traumas that run deep. There is work to be done to prepare this home to accommodate their special needs and to assist in their specialized care. Your gift has come, I believe, to help with that work."

Troy had reached to take Maggie's hand in his own. He knew this was a moment neither one would forget.

"Rich, I believe Maggie and Troy would agree, that it is an honor to share this opportunity with you."

"Yes, I whole heartedly agree." Troy added, "But, if I may, Rich, I'd like to make one suggestion."

"What is it?" Rich asked.

Troy looked first at Abe, and then at Rich, "Just make sure those veterans have a top-of-the-line pool table in the house that they can use anytime they want."

⌒

I should say, "well said," to all those
Who speak (Dharma) well,
And if I see someone doing good,
I should praise them and be well pleased.

I should discreetly talk about the qualities (of others)
And repeat those (that others) recount.
If my own good qualities are spoken about,
I should just know and be aware that I have them.

All deeds (of others) are the source of a joy
That would be rare even if it could be bought with money.
Therefore, I should be happy in finding this joy
In the good things that are done by others.
V. 75, 76, 77

How the Root of Kindness Works

Acknowledgments

Through a stroke of luck, I have the good fortune to live near Do Ngak Kunphen Ling in Redding, Connecticut where there are some very special monks who teach and patiently answer my steady stream of questions. In particular, I wish to thank Gyumed Khensur Rinpoche Lobsang Jampa, Geshe Lobsang Dhargey, and Venerable Jampa Gyaltsen for generously helping to clarify some of the more subtle and sensitive aspects of Shantideva's teachings for me while writing *How the Root of Kindness Works*.

Many thanks to John and Clare Cerullo at Diamond Cutter Press. John's knowledge and understanding of Master Shantideva's *Guide to the Bodhisattva's Way of Life* has guided the writing of this book. It would be an understatement to say I would be lost without his guidance. Clare's sensitive touch as editor and designer is responsible for having turned the pages of manuscript into the book you now hold in your hands.

A special thank you to my brother David Ettele who served in Vietnam and answered many questions that helped me to write about some of the aspects of active duty in the Vietnam War.

And lifetimes of gratitude to my sons Geoffrey and Daniel who are lovingly woven into the fibers of my heart and therefore an inspiration for all I do.